Spelling and Vocabulary Skills

Level 3

Teacher's Annotated Edition

A Division of The McGraw-Hill Companies

Columbus, Ohio

www.sra4kids.com

SRA/McGraw-Hill

A Division of The **McGraw·Hill** *Companies*

Copyright © 2002 by SRA/McGraw-Hill.

All rights reserved. Except as permitted under the United States
Copyright Act, no part of this publication may be reproduced or
distributed in any form or by any means, or stored in a database
or retrieval system, without the prior written permission of the
publisher, unless otherwise indicated.

Send all inquiries to:
SRA/McGraw-Hill
8787 Orion Place
Columbus, OH 43240-4027

Printed in the United States of America.

ISBN 0-07-571103-6

4 5 6 7 8 9 POH 07 06 05 04

Table of Contents

Curr Text Reading Sr11 Grade 3
Adams, Marilyn
Open court reading

Unit 1   Friendship

Lesson 1 *"Gloria Who Might Be My Best Friend"*
Vocabulary: Vocabulary Strategies **2**
Spelling: The /a/ Sound **4**

Lesson 2 *"Angel Child, Dragon Child"*
Vocabulary: Context Clues **6**
Spelling: The /e/ Sound **8**

Lesson 3 *"The Tree House"*
Vocabulary: Word Structure **10**
Spelling: The /i/ Sound **12**

Lesson 4 *"Rugby & Rosie"*
Vocabulary: Using a Dictionary **14**
Spelling: The /o/ Sound **16**

Lesson 5 *"Teammates"*
Vocabulary: Using a Thesaurus **18**
Spelling: The /u/ Sound **20**

Lesson 6 *"The Legend of Damon and Pythias"*
Vocabulary: Word Maps **22**
Spelling: Short-Vowel Sounds **24**

Unit 2   City Wildlife

Lesson 1 *"The Boy Who Didn't Believe in Spring"*
Vocabulary: Antonyms **26**
Spelling: The /âr/ and /ar/ Sounds **28**

Lesson 2 *"City Critters: Wild Animals Live in Cities, Too"*
Vocabulary: Categories **30**
Spelling: The /er/ and /or/ Sounds **32**

Lesson 3 *"Make Way for Ducklings"*
Vocabulary: Synonyms **34**
Spelling: The Final /əl/ Sound **36**

Lesson 4 *"Urban Roosts: Where Birds Nest in the City"*
Vocabulary: Word Concept **38**
Spelling: The /ow/ Sound **40**

Lesson 5 *"Two Days in May"*
Vocabulary: Homophones **42**
Spelling: The /oi/ Sound **44**

Lesson 6 *"Secret Place"*
Vocabulary: Unit 2 Review **46**
Spelling: Unit 2 Review **48**

Unit 3   Imagination

Lesson 1 *"Through Grandpa's Eyes"*
Vocabulary: Base Word Families **50**
Spelling: The /ā/ Sound **52**

Lesson 2 *"The Cat Who Became a Poet"*
Vocabulary: Suffixes **54**
Spelling: The /ē/ Sound **56**

Lesson 3 *"A Cloak for the Dreamer"*
Vocabulary: Prefixes **58**
Spelling: The /ī/ Sound **60**

Lesson 4 *"Picasso"*
Vocabulary: Multiple Meanings. **62**
Spelling: The /ō/ Sound. **64**

Lesson 5 *"The Emperor's New Clothes"*
Vocabulary: Shades of Meaning **66**
Spelling: The /ū/ and /o͞o/ Sounds **68**

Lesson 6 *"Roxaboxen"*
Vocabulary: Unit 3 Review **70**
Spelling: Unit 3 Review **72**

Unit 4 Money

Lesson 1 *"A New Coat for Anna"*
Vocabulary: Base Word Families. **74**
Spelling: Double Consonants **76**

Lesson 2 *"Alexander, Who Used to Be Rich Last Sunday"*
Vocabulary: The Suffix *-ly*. **78**
Spelling: Final Double Consonants **80**

Lesson 3 *"Kids Did It! in Business"*
Vocabulary: Business and Technology Words **82**
Spelling: Contractions **84**

Lesson 4 *"The Cobbler's Song"*
Vocabulary: The Endings *-ed* and *-ing*. **86**
Spelling: Adding *-ed* and *-ing* **88**

Lesson 5 *"Four Dollars and Fifty Cents"*
Vocabulary: Compound Words **90**
Spelling: Adding *-s* or *-es* to Make Plurals **92**

Lesson 6 *"The Go-Around Dollar"*
Vocabulary: Money Words. **94**
Spelling: Compound Words **96**

Lesson 7 *"Uncle Jed's Barbershop"*
Vocabulary: Unit 4 Review **98**
Spelling: Unit 4 Review **100**

Unit 5 Storytelling

Lesson 1 *"A Story A Story"*
Vocabulary: Categories. **102**
Spelling: Consonant Blends **104**

Lesson 2 *"Oral History"*
Vocabulary: Homographs **106**
Spelling: The /n/ and /r/ Sounds **108**

Lesson 3 *"Storm in the Night"*
Vocabulary: The Suffixes *-ly* and *-ness* **110**
Spelling: Words with *lf*, *mb*, and *tch* **112**

Lesson 4 *"Carving the Pole"*
Vocabulary: Cultural Words **114**
Spelling: The /ə/ Sound. **116**

Lesson 5 *"The Keeping Quilt"*
Vocabulary: Words with Foreign Origins **118**
Spelling: The /kw/ and /skw/ Sounds **120**

Lesson 6 *"Johnny Appleseed"*
Vocabulary: Prefixes **122**
Spelling: The /s/ and /j/ Sounds **124**

Lesson 7 *"Aunt Flossie's Hats (and Crab Cakes Later)"*
Vocabulary: Unit 5 Review **126**
Spelling: Unit 5 Review **128**

Unit 6 Country Life

Lesson 1 *"The Country Mouse and the City Mouse"*
Vocabulary: Antonyms **130**
Spelling: Irregular Plurals **132**

Lesson 2 *"Heartland"*
Vocabulary: Synonyms **134**
Spelling: Double Consonants + *y* **136**

Lesson 3 *"Leah's Pony"*
Vocabulary: Homophones **138**
Spelling: Words with *-er* and *-est* **140**

Lesson 4 *"Cows in the Parlor: A Visit to a Dairy Farm"*
Vocabulary: Categories **142**
Spelling: Words with Latin Roots **144**

Lesson 5 *"Just Plain Fancy"*
Vocabulary: Base Word Families **146**
Spelling: Words with Greek Roots **148**

Lesson 6 *"What Ever Happened to the Baxter Place?"*
Vocabulary: Word Concept **150**
Spelling: Words with Foreign Origins **152**

Lesson 7 *"If you're not from the prairie . . ."*
Vocabulary: Unit 6 Review **154**
Spelling: Unit 6 Review **156**

Vocabulary Rules **158**

Spelling Strategies **162**

Spelling Rules **164**

UNIT 1 Friendship • **Lesson 1** *Gloria Who Might Be My Best Friend*

Vocabulary Strategies

As you read, you may see words you do not understand. You may not know these words, but there are many ways to learn what they mean. Here are some ideas:

> Read to see if the sentence gives you clues.
> Plug the word into a possible sentence.
> Look the word up in a dictionary.

 **What are three other ways you could learn more about the meaning of an unfamiliar word?**

possible answers: Look in an Encyclopedia. Check the Internet. Look in a Thesaurus. Ask your parents. Read the sentences around the word to see if they describe what the word means.

1. Plug the word *minute* into the sentence below.

The cookies needed to bake for one more ___minute___ in the oven.

2. Can you find clues from the sentence that help you know what the word *minute* means? Write what you think the word *minute* means.

possible answer: time to cook

3. What is one definition for *minute* in a dictionary?
Write it below:

"60 seconds" "a short space of time"

UNIT 1 Friendship • **Lesson 1** *Gloria Who Might Be My Best Friend*

▶**Vocabulary Strategies**

Practice

Circle the word that makes sense in each sentence. When thinking about each word, read the sentence aloud. Does it sound right?

squawked
mustache
4. The thirsty girl drank a   minute   milkshake.
garage
(strawberry)

**Example:
The thirsty girl drank a *mustache* milkshake. The thirsty girl drank a *strawberry* milkshake.**

garage
squawked
5. Under his nose, the man's   strawberry   was long and black.
(mustache)
minute

(squawked)
minute
6. The angry bird   garage   at the dog under the tree.
strawberry
mustache

squawked
strawberry
7. "I'll be there in a   mustache   !" shouted the bus driver.
(minute)
garage

(garage)
minute
8. Out in the   strawberry,   the old car sat waiting for repairs.   squawked
mustache

UNIT 1 **Friendship • Lesson 1** *Gloria Who Might Be My Best Friend*

The /a/ Sound

Word List

1. path
2. lamp
3. damp
4. crash
5. plant
6. math
7. trash
8. stamp
9. hatbox
10. have

Selection Words

11. grass
12. rags
13. back
14. black
15. that

Pattern Study

The /a/ sound is a short-vowel sound.
The /a/ sound is always spelled with the letter *a* at the beginning or in the middle of a word. There are few words that end in the /a/ sound spelled *a*. The /a/ sound is often followed by one or two consonants, as in *ba<u>t</u>* or *ba<u>th</u>*.

▶ Find the spelling words with the /a/ sound that match the spelling patterns below.
Order of answers may vary.
The /a/ sound is followed by two consonants:

1. path
2. back
3. crash
4. stamp
5. math
6. damp
7. trash
8. grass
9. rags
10. lamp
11. plant
12. black
13. hatbox

The /a/ sound is followed by one consonant:

14. that
15. have

The /a/ Sound

Strategies

 Consonant-Substitution Strategy
Substitute the letter or letters shown for the underlined consonant to spell a new word with the /a/ sound.

16. grass   (l)   **glass**

17. back   (tr)   **track**

18. black   (s)   **slack**

19. rags   (fl)   **flags**

 Visualization Strategy Circle the correct spelling for each word with the /a/ sound. Write the correct spelling on the line.

20. (plant) plannt   **plant**

21. hav   (have)   **have**

22. bak   (back)   **back**

 Meaning Strategy Write the spelling word that makes sense in each sentence.

23. Sunlight helps a ____**plant**____ grow.

24. Some ____**trash**____ can be recycled.

25. Ladybugs are often red with ____**black**____ spots.

26. A ____**lamp**____ lights up a dark room.

> **Exceptions**
> The **a_e** pattern usually makes the /ā/ sound, as in *save* and *hate*. In the word *have*, it makes the /a/ sound.

SPELLING

UNIT 1 Friendship • **Lesson 2** *Angel Child, Dragon Child*

►Context Clues

> **Context clues** are words, or sentences, before or after a hard word. They help you figure out what the hard word might mean.
>
> She ate the delicious <u>bagel</u> for breakfast.
>
> ►Unfamiliar word: *bagel*
>
> ►Clue Words in the sentence: *ate, delicious, breakfast*
>
> ►Meaning: A *bagel* must be something good to eat for breakfast.

Read the sentence below from page 29 of "Angel Child, Dragon Child."

Somewhere, a loud bell <u>jangled</u>.

List two clue words within the sentence that can help you understand the meaning of *jangled*.

1. _____

2. _____

possible clue words: bell, loud

UNIT 1   Friendship • **Lesson 2** *Angel Child, Dragon Child*

►**Context Clues**

Practice

Find the five vocabulary words below in "Angel Child, Dragon Child." Read the sentence in which each word is found. Think about the context clues you can find in the sentence. Try to find two or three clue words from each sentence that might help you learn the meaning of the word.

Answers will vary.

Vocabulary Word		**Clue Words**
3. jangled	(page 29)	bell, loud, school
4. chant	(page 29)	said, taught
5. trilled	(page 32)	bell, time, home
6. chives	(page 33)	leaves, rice, noodles
7. margins	(page 40)	sheet, paper, crayoned

VOCABULARY

The /e/ Sound

Word List

1. deck
2. tent
3. spent
4. fence
5. head
6. dead
7. bread
8. desk
9. thread
10. sweater

Selection Words

11. edge
12. bell
13. next
14. send
15. them

Pattern Study

The /e/ sound is a short-vowel sound. The /e/ sound can be spelled *e* and *ea*, as is *bed* or *head*.

▶ Sort the spelling words under the word with the same /e/ sound spelling pattern.
Order of answers may vary.

lead

1. head
2. dead
3. bread
4. thread
5. sweater

test

6. tent
7. spent
8. fence
9. desk
10. edge
11. bell
12. next
13. send
14. them
15. deck

SPELLING

▶ **The /e/ Sound**

Strategies

Rhyming Strategy Write the spelling word or words that rhyme with each word below. Listen for the /e/ sound in each word.

16. went __tent__ __spent__

17. lead __bread__ __head__ __dead__ __thread__

18. neck __deck__

19. ledge __edge__

Visualization Strategy Circle the correct spelling for each word with the /e/ sound. Write the correct spelling on the line.

20. sweter (sweater) __sweater__

21. (next) naxt __next__

22. desck (desk) __desk__

Meaning Strategy Write the spelling word that makes sense in each sentence.

23. A stamp is needed to __send__ a letter.

24. You wear a __sweater__ to stay warm.

25. A baseball cap goes on your __head__.

> **Exceptions**
> The *ea* spelling pattern can also make the /ē/ sound, as in *meal* and *deal*.

UNIT I Friendship • **Lesson 3** *The Tree House*

Word Structure

> **Word structure** means the parts (like prefixes, suffixes, endings, and base words) that make up a word.
>
> Knowing the meaning of part of a word can help you begin to understand the meaning of the whole word.

 **Look at the word *hopelessness*.**

hopelessness

1. Circle the word *hope* and write it on the line.

(hope)lessness _____ **hope** _____

2. Circle the suffix *-less* in the word.

hope(less)ness

3. Circle the suffix *-ness* in the word.

hopeless(ness)

4. Find the meanings of *hope*, *-less*, and *-ness* in the dictionary and write them on the line.

hope: **to wish for something**

-less: **without**

-ness: **state of being**

5. Think about how the parts of this word's structure combine to form the meaning of the word.

► **Word Structure**

VOCABULARY

Practice

Look at the Vocabulary Skill Words *shutters,
markers, hinges,* and *paintbrush.* Remember
what you have learned about breaking down
the structure of a word. Write the base words
you can find within each vocabulary word
from "The Tree House."

Vocabulary Word		Base Words
6. shutters	(page 48)	shut
7. markers	(page 49)	mark
8. paintbrush	(page 49)	paint
		brush
9. hinges	(page 48)	hinge

UNIT I Friendship • **Lesson 3** *The Tree House*

The /i/ Sound

Word List

1. pick
2. risk
3. film
4. grip
5. brick
6. give
7. stitch
8. finish
9. trick
10. live

Selection Words

11. window
12. visit
13. lift
14. with
15. into

Pattern Study

The /i/ sound is a short-vowel sound. The /i/ sound is spelled with the letter *i* at the beginning and in the middle of words.

The /i/ sound is often followed by one or two consonants, as in *fit* and *pick*.

▶ Find the spelling words with the /i/ sound that match the spelling patterns below.
Order of answers may vary.
The /i/ sound followed by two consonants:

1. pick
2. lift
3. brick
4. risk
5. with
6. trick
7. film
8. finish
9. window
10. into

The /i/ sound followed by one consonant:

11. grip
12. visit
13. live
14. give

UNIT 1   Friendship • **Lesson 3** *The Tree House*

▶ **The /i/ Sound**

Strategies

 Consonant-Substitution Strategy Substitute the letter or letters shown for the underlined letter or letters to spell a new word with the /i/ sound.

15. fil<u>m</u>   (l)   <u>**fill**</u>

16. gri<u>p</u>   (d)   <u>**grid**</u>

17. tri<u>ck</u>   (m)   <u>**trim**</u>

18. <u>w</u>ith   (sh)   <u>**wish**</u>

19. <u>l</u>ift   (dr)   <u>**drift**</u>

 Meaning Strategy Write the spelling word that fits the meaning clue.

20. ____**brick**____ a hard, rectangular object used to make houses

21. ____**finish**____ the end, to end, to complete

22. ____**window**____ something to look through, an opening in a wall

23. ____**pick**____ to choose

24. ____**grip**____ to hold on to, grab

> ### Exceptions
> The *i_e* spelling pattern usually makes the /ī/ sound, as in *dive* or *hive*. In the words *give* and *live*, it makes the /i / sound.

SPELLING

Name _____ Date _____

Using a Dictionary

Did you know that the first English dictionary was written hundreds of years ago?

A dictionary is a tool that can help you learn to spell, define, and write the different forms of a word. The words in a dictionary are in alphabetical order. Knowing the first couple of letters in a word can help you find the word in a dictionary.

 **Try It!**   **Take a look at the dictionary page below:**

---

bird / brown

bird /bûrd/ *n.* an animal that has wings, two legs, and a body covered with feathers.
birthday /bûrth•dā/ *n.* **1.** the day on which a person is born. **2.** the return each year of this day.
bite /bīt/ *v.* **bit, bit ten,** or **bit, bit ing. 1.** to seize, cut into, or pierce with the teeth.

bottle /bot•təl/ *n.* a container, usually made of glass or plastic, which holds liquids.
—*v.* **bot tled bot tling.** to put in bottles.
boy /boi/ n. a very young male child.
brainstorm /brān•storm/ *n.* a sudden, bright idea; inspiration.

---

1. Look for the word *birthday* in the sample dictionary page above.

2. Which word comes before *birthday* in the dictionary page? __**bird**__

3. Which word comes after *birthday* in the dictionary page? __**bite**__

4. Why do these words appear in this order? __**The entries in a**__
__**dictionary appear in alphabetical order.**__

5. How many definitions does the dictionary give for *birthday*?
__**two**__

►Using a Dictionary

Practice

Look at the Vocabulary Skill Words *chocolate*, *Labrador*, and *ordinary*. Remember that a dictionary is a tool for learning more about a word. Find these three words in a dictionary. On the lines below each word, write the definition the dictionary gives for the word. If there are many definitions in the dictionary, choose one of the meanings.

6. chocolate   (page 64 of "Rugby and Rosie")

definitions will vary

_____

_____

7. Labrador   (page 64 of "Rugby and Rosie")

definitions will vary

_____

_____

8. ordinary   (page 64 of "Rugby and Rosie")

definitions will vary

_____

_____

VOCABULARY

UNIT 1 Friendship • **Lesson 4** *Rugby and Rosie*

The /o/ Sound

Word List

1. rot
2. shot
3. crop
4. sock
5. clock
6. flock
7. body
8. spot
9. stocking
10. lobby

Selection Words

11. stop
12. got
13. lots
14. job
15. pond

Pattern Study

The /o/ sound is a short-vowel sound. The /o/ sound is spelled with the letter *o* at the beginning and in the middle of words. The /o/ sound is often followed by one or two consonants, as in *no<u>t</u>* and *soc<u>k</u>*.

▶ Find the spelling words with the /o/ sound that match the spelling patterns below.

Order of answers may vary.

The /o/ sound followed by one consonant:

1. got   4. crop   7. stop
2. shot   5. rot   8. body
3. job   6. spot

The /o/ sound followed by two consonants:

9. lots   12. clock   14. flock
10. pond   13. sock   15. stocking
11. lobby

The /o/ Sound

SPELLING

Strategies

Rhyming Strategy Write the spelling word or words that rhyme with each word below. Listen to the /o/ sound in each word.

14. mop   __stop__   __crop__

15. rock   __sock__   __clock__   __flock__

16. rot   __shot__   __spot__   __got__

17. hobby   __lobby__

Consonant-Substitution Strategy Substitute the letter or letters shown for the underlined letter or letters to spell a new word with the /o/ sound.

18. sho̲t   (p)   __shop__

19. c̲rop   (d)   __drop__

20. s̲t̲ocking   (r)   __rocking__

Meaning Strategy Write the spelling word that fits the meaning clue.

21. __clock__ an instrument that tells time

22. __rot__ spoil

23. __pond__ a small body of water

Name _____ Date _____

Using a Thesaurus

A thesaurus is a tool that lists the synonyms for a word. Like the words in a dictionary, the words in a thesaurus are in alphabetical order.

A **synonym** is a word that has the same, or nearly the same, meaning as another word.

mad is a synonym for *angry*

Both words have the same basic meaning. If you did not know the meaning of *angry* but you knew the word *mad*, then knowing that they are synonyms would help you understand that their meanings are the same.

 **Try It!**   **Look for the word *extraordinary* in a thesaurus. (This word is found on page 83 of "Teammates.")**

1. How did you find *extraordinary* in the thesaurus?

I found the *e* section of the thesaurus and then looked for words starting with *extra*-.

2. List three synonyms for the word *extraordinary*.

outstanding   **remarkable**   **unusual**

UNIT I Friendship • **Lesson 5** *Teammates*

Practice

Look at the vocabulary words below. Find these three words in a thesaurus. On the first line, write two of the synonyms the thesaurus gives for the word. Think of one or two more synonyms you could use to describe the word. Write those words on the second line.

3. segregation   (page 83 of "Teammates")

thesaurus: **isolation**   **separation**

2 more: **discriminatio**   **exclusion**

4. apathetic   (page 85 of "Teammates")

thesaurus: **detached**   **insensible**

2 more: **uncaring**   **unemotional**

5. hostility   (page 88 of "Teammates")

thesaurus: **warlike**   **aggressive**

2 more: **hatred**   **anger**

UNIT 1 Friendship • **Lesson 5** *Teammates*

The /u/ Sound

Word List

1. dusk
2. blush
3. crust
4. thump
5. shut
6. dump
7. scrub
8. pump
9. buff
10. buzz

Selection Words

11. but
12. just
13. bus
14. upon
15. much

Pattern Study

The /u/ sound is a short-vowel sound. The /u/ sound is spelled with the letter *u* at the beginning and in the middle of words. The /u/ sound is often followed by one or two consonants, as in *bu<u>s</u>* and *mu<u>st</u>*.

▶ Find the spelling words with the /u/ sound that match the spelling patterns below.

The /u/ sound followed by one consonant:

1. bus _____ 3. but _____   **Order of**
2. scrub _____ 4. shut _____ **answers may vary.**

The /u/ sound followed by two consonants:

5. dusk _____   9. much _____ 13. thump _____
6. just _____   10. crust _____ 14. buff _____
7. blush _____ 11. pump _____
8. dump _____   12. buzz _____

The /u/ sound found at the beginning of a word:

15. upon _____

UNIT I Friendship • **Lesson 5** *Teammates*

▶ **The /u/ Sound**

Strategies

Vowel-Substitution Strategy Substitute the vowel *u* for the underlined vowel in each word to spell a new word with the /u/ sound. Write each new word on the line.

16. d<u>e</u>sk **dusk**

17. cr<u>e</u>st **crust**

18. sh<u>o</u>t **shut**

Rhyming Strategy Write the spelling word or words that rhyme with each word below. Listen to the /u/ sound in each word.

19. must **just**   **crust**

20. bump **thump**   **dump**   **pump**

21. fuzz **buzz**

Order of answers may vary.

Visualization Strategy Circle and then write the spelling word that is spelled correctly.

22. (upon)   apon   **upon**

23. bluosh   (blush)   **blush**

24. thummp   (thump)   **thump**

25. (scrub)   scrubb   **scrub**

SPELLING

UNIT I Friendship • **Lesson 6** *The Legend of Damon and Pythias*

Word Maps

A "word map" is a way of organizing the information about a word to fully understand the meaning of the word. Here is a word map for the word *army* from page 96 of "The Legend of Damon and Pythias."

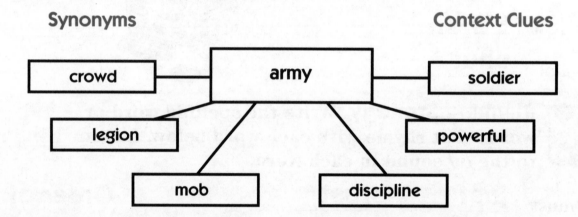

Synonyms   **Context Clues**

crowd — army — soldier

legion   powerful

mob   discipline

 **Think about the word *traitor* from page 101 of "The Legend of Damon and Pythias."**

1. Find three synonyms for the word *traitor* in a thesaurus.

betrayer   **double-crosser**   **enemy**

2. Find three context clues from the story that describe *traitor*.

prison   **crime**   **rebel**

3. On a separate piece of paper, draw a word map for the word *traitor* with the information you have found. **Word maps will vary.**

▶**Word Maps**

VOCABULARY

Practice

Find the word *astonished* on page 102 of "The Legend of Damon & Pythias." You will make a word map for the word *astonish*.

4. Look in a thesaurus to find three synonyms for the word *astonish*.

    amaze   **astound**   **startle**

5. Read sentences around the word *astonish* to find three clues for what the word means.

    can't believe   **curious**   **What**

6. Write the word *astonish* in a center box. Draw a word map for the word *astonish*, using the words above. Look at the word map on page 22 to help you.
Word maps will vary.

Short-Vowel Sounds

Word List

1. brand
2. candy
3. plan
4. hobby
5. best
6. read
7. us
8. top
9. jump
10. send

Selection Words

11. tell
12. prison
13. last
14. robbers
15. struggle

Pattern Study

Short-vowel sounds are easy to spell.
/a / is spelled *a*   /o/ is spelled *o*
/e/ is spelled *e* and *ea*   /u/ is spelled *u*
/i/ is spelled *i*

▶ Sort the spelling words under the word with the same short-vowel sound.
Order of answers may vary.

tr<u>a</u>sh

1. brand   3. plan

2. candy

h<u>e</u>lp

4. best   6. send

5. read

sh<u>o</u>p

7. hobby   8. top

b<u>u</u>mp

9. us   10. jump

▶ **Short-Vowel Sounds**

Strategies

Visualization Strategy Circle the correct spelling for each word with a short vowel sound. Write the correct spelling on the line.

11. hoby ⟨hobby⟩ **hobby** _____

12. ⟨candy⟩ kandy **candy** _____

13. rede ⟨read⟩ **read** _____

14. prisin ⟨prison⟩ **prison** _____

15. robers ⟨robbers⟩ **robbers** _____

Proofreading Strategy Correct the spelling of the underlined word in each sentence. Write the correct spelling on the line.

16. Kangaroos can <u>jemp</u> long distances. ____ **jump** ____

17. The gold medal goes to the <u>bost</u> athlete in the Olympics.
____ **best** ____

18. Ranchers <u>brend</u> their cattle's hides with a hot iron.
____ **brand** ____

19. Some people <u>tel</u> stories with morals called fables.
____ **tell** ____

20. Two teams <u>strugle</u> during the game tug-of-war.
____ **struggle** ____

SPELLING

UNIT 2 City Wildlife • **Lesson I** • *The Boy Who Didn't Believe in Spring*

▶ Antonyms

Antonyms are words that have opposite meanings. Sometimes a thesaurus or dictionary will include some antonyms of a word after the list of synonyms.

happy and *sad* are antonyms

Example polite

Antonyms for *polite:* rude, inconsiderate, thoughtless

Synonyms for *polite:* courteous, mannerly
                      being considerate and thoughtful

Notice *hollered* on page 123 of "The Boy Who Didn't Believe in Spring." List one or more words that mean the opposite of the word *hollered*. Look in a thesaurus to find antonyms if you have trouble thinking of your own examples.

Antonyms for *hollered:*

1. __whispered_____

2. __sighed_____

3. __mumbled_____

Antonyms

Practice

Find the word *slowly* on page 121 of "The Boy Who Didn't Believe in Spring." Read the sentence in which the word is found. Remember, the context clues in the sentences around the word can help you learn the meaning of the word *slowly*.

4. Write two words that are context clues from the sentence:

walked _____ **tiptoeing** _____

5. Write two words that you think might be antonyms for the word *slowly*:

fast _____ **quickly** _____

6. Look in a thesaurus to find two more antonyms that will further describe the opposite meanings of *slowly*.

rapidly _____ **swiftly** _____

VOCABULARY

Name _____ Date _____

The /âr/ and /ar/ Sounds

Word List

1. bare
2. chair
3. dare
4. wear
5. fare
6. fair
7. glare
8. hair
9. bear
10. share

Selection Words

11. air
12. car
13. dark
14. apartments
15. started

Pattern Study

The /âr/ sound can be spelled many ways:

are as in *care*   *air* as in *hair*
ear as in *bear*

The /ar/ sound is spelled *ar* as in *jar*.

▶ Sort the spelling words under the word with the same /âr/ or /ar/ sound spelling pattern.
order of answers may vary

/âr/ as in *care*

1. bare   3. dare   5. fare

2. glare   4. share

/âr/ as in *tear*

6. wear   7. bear

/âr/ as in *stairs*

8. hair   10. fair

9. chair   11. air

/ar/ as in *jar*

12. car   14. dark

13. apartments   15. started

▶ The /âr/ and /ar/ **Sounds**

SPELLING

Strategies

Consonant-Substitution Strategy
Substitute the consonant in parentheses for the underlined consonant in each word. Write the new word on the line.

16. <u>d</u>ark   (b)   **bark** _____

17. <u>c</u>ar   (t)   **tar** _____

18. s<u>h</u>are   (c)   **scare** _____

Visualization Strategy
Circle the correct spelling for each word. Write the correct spelling on the line.

19. shair   (share)   **share** _____

20. (bare)   bair   **bare** _____

21. weare   (wear)   **wear** _____

Meaning Strategy
Write the spelling word that makes sense in each sentence.

22. A royal _____ **chair** _____ is called a throne.

23. It is not _____ **fair** _____ to copy someone else's homework.

24. Most races are _____ **started** _____ by the word, "go."

Categories

You can learn a lot more about a word by sorting it into categories. A **category** is a grouping of similar things. A word map can help you categorize a word, such as *pie*.

Example

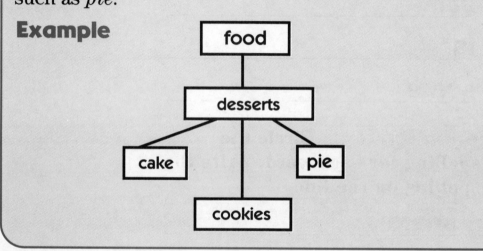

 **Think about the word *skyscraper* from page 127 of "City Critters." What is a skyscraper? In what category could it be included?**

Fill in the blanks in the word map to show the specific meaning of the word *skyscraper*.

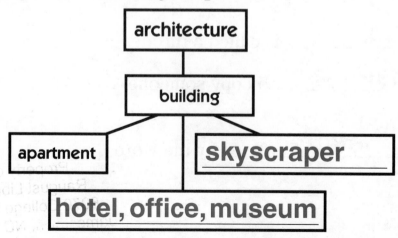

UNIT 2 **City Wildlife • Lesson 2 •** *City Critters*

▶**Categories**

VOCABULARY

Practice

Find the words *pollution, waste,* and *exhaust* on page 128 of "City Critters." Can you think of how these words could be connected? Fill in the correct blanks of the word map below with the words *pollution, litter,* and *exhaust.*

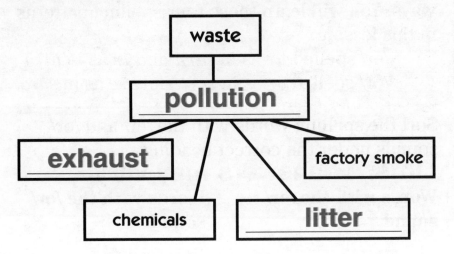

1. What is a type of *waste?* <u>pollution</u>

2. What are some things that are a result of *pollution?*

   <u>exhaust</u>   <u>litter</u>   <u>chemicals</u>

3. Look up the word *exhaust* in a dictionary. What is *exhaust?*

   <u>possible answer: the gases that</u>

   <u>come out of a car's engine</u>

Name _____ Date _____

The /er/ and /or/ Sounds

Word List

1. porch
2. nurse
3. fort
4. hurry
5. sport
6. hurt
7. curb
8. tore
9. storm
10. burn

Selection Words

11. urban
12. forget
13. bird
14. short
15. before

Pattern Study

The /er/ and /or/ sounds can be spelled many ways. You will learn these four spelling patterns in this lesson:

/er/ spelled *ur* as in *turn* and *ir* as in *bird*

/or/ spelled *or* as in *sort* and *ore* as in *sore*

▶ Sort the spelling words with the /er/ and /or/ sounds under the correct heading. **Order of answers may vary.**

Words with the /er/ sound

1. burn
2. curb
3. hurt
4. hurry
5. nurse
6. urban
7. bird

Words with the /or/ sound

8. porch
9. fort
10. sport
11. storm
12. tore
13. forget
14. short
15. before

UNIT 2 City Wildlife • **Lesson 2** • *City Critters*

▶ The /er/ and /or/ Sounds

Strategies

Visualization Strategy Circle and then write the spelling word that is spelled correctly.

16. burd   (bird)   bird

17. (fort)   foret   fort

18. irban   (urban)   urban

19. (tore)   tor   tore

20. ferget   (forget)   forget

Rhyming Strategy Write the spelling word or words that rhyme with each word below. Listen to the /er/ and /or/ sounds in each word.

21. sort   sport   fort

22. turn   burn   Order of answers may vary.

23. torch   porch

Meaning Strategy Write the correct spelling word next to the meaning clue.

24. a game, a physical activity   sport

25. to damage with heat or fire   burn

26. a person in the medical profession   nurse

UNIT 2 **City Wildlife • Lesson 3** *Make Way for Ducklings*

Synonyms

Synonyms are words with the same or nearly the same meaning. A dictionary or a thesaurus can help you find synonyms for many words.

yell, *scream*, and *shout* are synonyms

If you know a synonym for a word, you can begin to understand the meaning of the word by replacing the synonym for the word in the sentence.

Example Cheerleaders <u>yell</u> and clap for the team.
Cheerleaders <u>scream</u> and clap for the team.
Cheerleaders <u>shout</u> and clap for the team.

 **Try It!** **Think about the word *responsibility* from page 140 of "Make Way for Ducklings."**

1. Look in a thesaurus or a dictionary to find two synonyms for the word *responsibility*.
   possible synonyms: duty, job, concern
   _____ _____

2. Fill in the blanks below with your two synonyms for the word *responsibility*. Read each sentence to see if the word makes sense. If the words are synonyms, they should give each sentence a similar meaning.
   His <u>responsibility</u> is to feed the dog each day.

   His __**possible: duty**__ is to feed the dog each day.

   His __**possible: job**__ is to feed the dog each day.

UNIT 2 City Wildlife • **Lesson 3** *Make Way for Ducklings*

Practice

Find the word *beckoned* on page 142 of "Make Way for Ducklings." Read the sentence in which the word is found. Knowing synonyms for the word can help you learn what the word means in the sentence.

3. Write some words from the sentence that could be context clues to help you learn the meaning of the word.

possible answers: raised, hand, to cross

4. Look up two synonyms for the word *beckoned* in a thesaurus or a dictionary.

possible answers: signed, signaled, motioned

5. Substitute your synonyms for the word *beckoned* in the sentence below:

Michael <u>beckoned</u> for Mrs. Mallard to cross the street.

Michael _____**signaled**_____ for Mrs. Mallard to cross the street.

Michael _____**motioned**_____ for Mrs. Mallard to cross the street.

6. Use the word *beckoned* in a sentence that shows what *beckoned* means.

Answers will vary.

_____

_____

VOCABULARY

The Final /əl/ Sound

Word List

1. candle
2. handle
3. tangle
4. jungle
5. marble
6. apple
7. bubble
8. bottle
9. jingle
10. pebble

Selection Words

11. people
12. turtles
13. little
14. waddle
15. whistle

Pattern Study

The final /əl/ sound can be spelled many ways. This lesson teaches the /əl/ sound spelled *le*. The letter *e* is silent. Many times, a double consonant comes before a final /əl/ sound spelled *le*, such as the *tt* in the word *little*. Many words with the final /əl/ sound have the spelling patterns **n_le** or **r_le**.

▶ Sort the spelling words with the final /əl/ sound under the correct heading. **Order of answers may vary.**

Words with a double consonant before *le*:

1. apple
2. bubble
3. bottle
4. pebble
5. little
6. waddle

Words with the **n_le** spelling pattern:

7. candle
8. jungle
9. handle
10. jingle
11. tangle

Words with the **r_le** spelling pattern:

12. marble
13. turtles

► **The Final /əl/ Sound**

SPELLING

Strategies Order of answers may vary.

Rhyming Strategy Write the spelling
word or words that rhyme with each
word below. Listen to the final /əl/ sound
in each word.

14. angle   **tangle**

15. whittle   **little**

16. single   **jingle**

Meaning Strategy Write the spelling
word that correctly completes each
sentence.

17. Gorillas live deep in the **jungle**.

18. A **candle** is lit on top of a birthday cake.

19. You should **handle** a baby very carefully.

20. Many **people** like to go to the movies.

Visualization Strategy Circle and then
write the spelling word that is spelled
correctly.

21. appil   (apple)   **apple**

22. (bottle)   botle   **bottle**

23. littel   (little)   **little**

24. (jungle)   jungul   **jungle**

25. (bubble)   buble   **bubble**

Word Concept

> The **concept** of a word is an idea that a word stands for. You can discover the concept of a word by thinking of related words or finding clues within the context.
>
> **Example** pigeon (from page 148 of "Urban Roosts")
> Related Words: dove, sparrow
> Context Clues: flying, flocks, roost
> Concept: a *pigeon* is a bird

 **Read the sentence containing the word *debris* from page 150 of "Urban Roosts."**

1. List two words from the sentence that could be related to the word *debris*.
possible answers: sticks, twigs

_____   _____

2. List two or more context clues found in the sentence or surrounding sentences that could relate to the word *debris*.

possible answers: nest, roost, flimsy platform

_____

3. What could be the concept, or general idea, of the word *debris*? **answers will vary: debris is trash or litter or found objects**

_____

If you want to find the specific meaning of the word *debris*, look up the definition in the dictionary.

▶**Word Concept**

VOCABULARY

{Practice}

Find the word *migrate* on page 151 of "Urban Roosts." Read the sentence in which the word is found. Discovering the concept of the word can help you learn what the word means in the sentence.

4. Write some words from the sentence that could be context clues to help you learn the concept of the word *migrate.* **possible answers: sparrows, finches, throughout the year**

5. Find the word *migrate* in a dictionary and write the definition below: **possible definition: to travel from one place to another**

6. Thinking about the context clues and the definition, list some related words for the word *migrate.* **answers will vary: birds, travel, move, go, fly away**

7. How does the concept, or general idea, of the word *migrate* apply to the sentence?

   answers will vary: to migrate is to

   move, so the birds do not move each

   year, they stay in the same place

The /ow/ Sound

Pattern Study

The /ow/ sound can be spelled *ow* and *ou*. The /ow/ sound is spelled *ou* more often than *ow*. The *ow* spelling pattern is often found at the end or near the end of a word, as in *town* or *cow*.

▶ Sort the spelling words with the /ow/ sound under the correct heading.
Order of answers may vary.
Words with /ow/ sound spelled *ou*:

1. mouse   5. bound   9. found
2. count   6. surrounds
3. mouth   7. house
4. south   8. throughout

Words with /ow/ sound spelled *ow*:

10. gown   13. frown
11. crown   14. crowd
12. brown   15. flowerpot

Word List

1. mouse
2. count
3. mouth
4. south
5. bound
6. gown
7. crown
8. brown
9. frown
10. crowd

Selection Words

11. flowerpot
12. house
13. throughout
14. surrounds
15. found

▶ **The /ow/ Sound**

Strategies Order of answers may vary.

Rhyming Strategy Write the spelling word or words that rhyme with each word below. Listen to the /ow/ sound in each word.

16. town ___gown___ ___crown___ ___brown___ ___frown___

17. round ___bound___ ___found___ ___surrounds___

Visualization Strategy Circle and then write the spelling word that is spelled correctly.

18. croun (crown) ___crown___

19. mowth (mouth) ___mouth___

20. (house) howse ___house___

21. (bound) bownd ___bound___

22. flourpot (flowerpot) ___flowerpot___

Meaning Strategy Write the correct spelling word next to its meaning clue.

23. the opposite of north ___south___

24. a home ___house___

25. a headpiece with jewels ___crown___

26. goes around ___surrounds___

27. a lot of people ___crowd___

Exception: In some words, *ow* can make the /ō/ sound, as in *blow*, *glow*, and *tow*.

SPELLING

Name _____ Date _____

Homophones

> Homophones are words that sound alike but have different spellings and different meanings. Think of the sound, spelling, and meaning of words when trying to decide if they are homophones.
>
> **Example** *sea* and *see* are homophones
> The words sound alike: *sea*   *see*
> The words have different spellings: *s<u>ea</u>*   *s<u>ee</u>*
> The words have different meanings:
>   *sea*   (a large body of salt water)
>   *see*   (to look at with the eyes)
>
> To spell homophones correctly, you must know the context in which the word is being used.
>   Fish swim in the *sea*.
>   People can *see* with their eyes.

 **Read the sentence containing the word *here* from page 166 of "Two Days in May."**

1. What is the meaning of *here* in the sentence?

<u>**possible answer: in this place, at the location**</u>

2. The words *here* and *hear* are homophones. How do you know?

Do they sound alike? ____**yes**____
Write the two different spellings:

here_____   **hear**_____

Write the two different definitions:
     here: <u>**at, in, or to this place**</u>
     hear: <u>**to receive sound through the ears**</u>

► **Homophones**

VOCABULARY

Practice

Remember, *homophones* are words that sound alike but have different spellings and different meanings.

The word *new* on page 166 of "Two Days in May" sounds like the word *knew*. Are these two words homophones? How do you know?

3. Spell the two words: _____ **new** _____ **knew** _____

4. What is the meaning of the word *new* in the context of the sentence in the story?

just grown, young, recently made

5. What does the word *knew* mean?

to have understood something, to have been certain

6. How could knowing that *know* and *knowledge* are related help you remember how to spell *knew?*

Both words start with *kn* as in *knew*, not *n* as in *new*.

UNIT 2   City Wildlife • **Lesson 5** *Two Days in May*

The /oi/ Sound

Pattern Study

The /oi/ sound can be spelled *oi* and *oy*. The *oi* spelling pattern is found at the beginning of words, such as *oil*, and in the middle of many words, such as *boil*. The *oy* spelling pattern is found at the end of words, such as *toy*, or at the end of a syllable, as in *royal*.

Word List

1. boy
2. enjoy
3. broil
4. oil
5. loyal
6. boil
7. soil
8. coil
9. coin
10. join
11. destroy
12. poison
13. royal
14. point

Selection Word

15. voices

▶ Sort the spelling words with the /oi/ sound under the correct heading.   **Order of answers may vary.**

Words with /oi/ spelled *oi*:

1. broil
2. oil
3. boil
4. soil
5. coil
6. coin
7. join
8. point
9. poison
10. voices

Words with /oi/ spelled *oy*:

11. boy
12. enjoy
13. destroy
14. royal
15. loyal

UNIT 2 City Wildlife • **Lesson 5** *Two Days in May*

► **The /oi/ Sound**

SPELLING

Strategies

Rhyming Strategy Write the spelling word or words that rhyme with each word below. Listen to the /oi/ sound in each word.

16. toy   **boy**   **enjoy**   **destroy**
17. foil   **broil**   **boil**   **coil**
    oil   **soil**
18. joint   **point**

Proofreading Strategy Each underlined word is misspelled. Write the correct spelling of the word on the line.

19. A fire can <u>destroi</u> a forest. **destroy**

20. A golden <u>coyn</u> is very valuable. **coin**

21. A fast way to cook chicken is to <u>broyl</u> it. **broil**

22. You <u>boyl</u> water to cook pasta. **boil**

23. Metal links <u>joyn</u> together to form a chain. **join**

24. Purple is considered a <u>roil</u> color. **royal**

> **Exception:**
> The *oy* spelling pattern for the /oi/ sound is found at the beginning of the word *oyster*.

UNIT 2   City Wildlife • **Lesson 6** *Secret Place*

Unit 2 Review

Remember, the concept of a word is the general idea for the word. You can discover the concept of a word by thinking of the related words or finding clues within the context.

Remember the example from "Urban Roosts": *pigeon* (page 148)

Related words:	dove, sparrow
Context Clues:	flying, flocks, roost
Concept:	a *pigeon* is a bird

 **Read the sentence containing the word *mallards* from page 185 of "Secret Place."**

1. List two words that you think could be related to the word *mallards*.
possible answers: birds, ducklings

_____   _____

2. List two or more context clues found in the sentence or surrounding sentences that could relate to the word *mallards*.

possible answers: green-winged, real, nest, feathers

3. What could be the concept, or general idea, of the word *mallards?*

answers will vary: mallards are a type of duck

If you want to find the specific meaning of the word *mallard*, look up the definition in the dictionary.

UNIT 2 City Wildlife • **Lesson 6** *Secret Place*

▶**Unit 2 Review**

VOCABULARY

Practice

Remember, a *category* is a group of related things.

Find the word *binoculars* on page 187 of "Secret Place." Can you think of how this word could be considered part of a certain type of group?

Fill in the correct blanks of the word map below with the word *binoculars* and other related words. Think of how the word *binoculars* relates to the other words on the map.

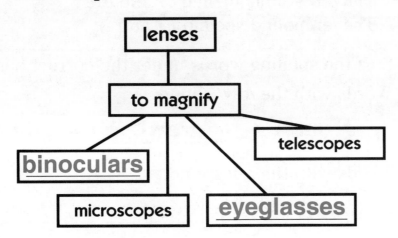

4. What are some types of lenses? _____
   telescopes, magnifying glasses, microscopes

5. What is one job a lens can perform? _____
   possible answer: it can magnify an object

6. Look up the word *binoculars* in a dictionary. What

   is the definition for *binoculars?* _____
   possible answer: two telescopes joined together for looking at objects in the distance

UNIT 2   City Wildlife • **Lesson 6** *Secret Place*

Unit 2 Review

Word List

1. noisy
2. choice
3. grouch
4. growl
5. puddle
6. dirt
7. pear
8. corner
9. rare
10. return

Selection Words

11. clouds
12. tangled
13. cradle
14. noise
15. jangled

Order of answers may vary.

Pattern Study

Remember the sound spellings from Unit 2:
The /ow/ sound spelled *ou* and *ow*.
The /oi/ sound spelled *oi* and *oy*.
The final /əl/ sound spelled *le*.
The /âr/ sound spelled *ear*, *are*, *air*.
The /or/ sound spelled *or* and *ore*.
The /er/ sound spelled *ur* and *ir*.

▶ Sort the spelling words under the correct heading.

Words with the /ow/ sound:

1. grouch   2. growl   3. clouds

Words with the /oi/ sound:

4. choice   5. noisy   6. noise

Words with the /əl/ sound:

7. puddle   9. jangled

8. tangled   10. cradle

Words with the /âr/ sound:

11. pear   12. rare

Words with the /er/ sound:

13. dirt   14. return   15. corner

UNIT 2 City Wildlife • **Lesson 6** *Secret Place*

▶ **Unit 2 Review**

SPELLING

Strategies

 Rhyming Strategy Write the spelling word or words that rhyme with each word below. Listen to the /ow/ or /oi/ sound in each word.

16. couch ___grouch___

17. voice ___choice___

18. howl ___growl___

 Visualization Strategy Circle and then write the spelling word that is spelled correctly.

19. paire　(pear)　___pear___

20. (return)　retern　___return___

21. craydel　(cradle)　___cradle___

22. (dirt)　durt　___dirt___

 Meaning Strategy Write the correct spelling word next to its meaning clue.

23. a small pool of water ___puddle___

24. in a knot ___tangled___

25. rang, like a bell ___jangled___

UNIT 3 Imagination • **Lesson 1** *Through Grandpa's Eyes*

Base Word Families

> A *base word* is a word that can have prefixes, suffixes, and endings added to it. *Base word families* are all the forms you can make of that base word. If you know the meaning of the base word, you can begin to better understand the meanings of all its related words.
>
> Base Word   Base Word Family Words
> *wood*   *wooden*   *woodwork*
>   *woodpecker*   *woodwind*

 Notice the vocabulary words *sculpt* on page 204 and *sculpture* on page 205 of "Through Grandpa's Eyes." The words *sculpt* and *sculpture* are in the same *base word family*.

1. Circle the word *sculpt* hidden in the word *sculpture* below:

   (sculpt)ure

2. What does the base word *sculpt* mean in "Through Grandpa's Eyes"?

   possible answer: the action of modeling or shaping clay to make art

3. How does the word *sculpture* relate to its base word *sculpt?* What does the word *sculpture* mean?

   possible answer: A sculpture is the result of what you sculpt.

►**Base Word Families**

{ **Practice** }

Remember, words in the same base word family have related meanings to one base word. In the groups of words below, circle the two words that are in the same base word family. Write the base word of the group on the line.

Base Word

4. (direction) (director) dictionary   **direct** _____

5. clown (cloudy) (clouds)   **cloud** _____

6. (happiness) heart (unhappy)   **happy** _____

7. (sculpting) (sculpture) school   **sculpt** _____

8. (roomy) round (roommate)   **room** _____

9. (unwise) (wisdom) wire   **wise** _____

10. (saddened) sorrow (sadly)   **sad** _____

11. kept (cleaned) (cleanest)   **clean** _____

12. (angled) (triangle) apply   **angle** _____

13. wrap (written) (writing)   **write** _____

14. (nearly) (nearby) neat   **near** _____

15. (sunny) salty (sunrise)   **sun** _____

VOCABULARY

UNIT 3 Imagination • **Lesson I** *Through Grandpa's Eyes*

The /ā/ Sound

Aa

Word List

1. flame
2. blaze
3. spade
4. fail
5. mail
6. stain
7. play
8. away
9. plate
10. raise

Selection Words

11. clay
12. rain
13. awake
14. face
15. chain

Pattern Study

Long vowels sound like their letter names. The /ā/ sound can be spelled several ways.

a_e with a silent *e* as in *date*
ay at the end of a word as in *day*
ai in the middle of a word as in *tail*

▶ Sort the spelling words under the word with the same /ā/ sound spelling pattern.

h**a**t**e**

1. flame   3. spade   5. face
2. blaze   4. plate   6. awake

d**ay**

7. play   8. away   9. clay

t**ai**l

10. fail   12. stain   14. rain
11. mail   13. raise   15. chain

UNIT 3 Imagination • **Lesson I** *Through Grandpa's Eyes*

▶ **The /ā/ Sound**

Strategies

 Consonant-Substitution Strategy Substitute the given consonant for the underlined consonant in each word. Write the new word on the line.

16. <u>f</u>ail (p) **pail**

17. bla<u>z</u>e (m) **blame**

18. <u>r</u>ain (p) **pain**

19. <u>f</u>ace (r) **race**

20. s<u>p</u>ade (h) **shade**

 Visualization Strategy Circle the correct spelling for each word with the /ā/ sound. Write the correct spelling on the line.

21. (raise) rais **raise**

22. mayl (mail) **mail**

23. (away) awaye **away**

24. playt (plate) **plate**

 Meaning Strategy Write the spelling word next to its meaning clue.

25. not succeed, lose **fail**

26. your nose, eyes, chin, and mouth **face**

27. not asleep **awake**

SPELLING

UNIT 3 Imagination • **Lesson 2** *The Cat Who Became a Poet*

Suffixes

A *suffix* is added to the end of a word and changes the meaning of the word.

Base Word + Suffix (Meaning) = New Word New Meaning

good   + -ness ("state of") = goodness   "state of being good"

Some words can have two suffixes added.

The word *restlessness* has the suffixes **-ness** ("state of") and **-less** ("without").

rest + -less + -ness = restlessness "state of being without rest"

 **Try It!** **Notice how the vocabulary word *peacefulness*, on page 220 of "The Cat Who Became a Poet," has two suffixes.**

1. Circle the base word *peace* in the word *peacefulness* below:

(peace)fulness

2. The suffix *-ful* means "full of" or "having." Knowing this, what does the word *peaceful* mean?

possible answer: full of or having peace

3. Remember, the suffix *-ness* means "state of." What is the meaning of the word *peacefulness?*

possible answer: the state of being full of peace or the state of having peace

Suffixes

VOCABULARY

Practice

Remember, *suffixes* are added to the ends of words and change the meanings of words. Add the given suffixes to the words below. Then write the meaning of the new word. Look on page 54 if you need help with the meanings of the suffixes.

New Meaning answers may vary.

Word + Suffix = New Word			New Meaning
Example:			
kind	-ness	kindness	"state of being kind"
4. bright	-ness	**brightness**	**state of being bright**
5. force	-ful	**forceful**	**having force**
6. fear	-less	**fearless**	**without fear**
7. sweet	-ness	**sweetness**	**state of being sweet**
8. play	-ful	**playful**	**full of play**

Find the word *hopeless* on page 219 of "The Cat Who Became a Poet."

9. Knowing the meaning of the suffix *-less*, what does the word *hopeless* mean?

without hope

10. The suffix *-ful* can also be added to *hope* to make another word. Add *-ful* to *hope* and write the new meaning of the new word.

new word: **hopeful**   new meaning: **full of hope**

UNIT 3 Imagination • **Lesson 2** *The Cat Who Became a Poet*

The /ē/ Sound

Word List

1. neat
2. deal
3. clean
4. please
5. beast
6. keep
7. street
8. seen
9. easy
10. creek

Selection Words

11. eat
12. hearing
13. feel
14. real
15. tree

Pattern Study

Long vowels sound like their letter names. The /ē/ sound can be spelled many ways.

    e_e with a silent *e* as in *these*

    y at the end of a word as in *happy*

    ee at the end or in the middle of a word as in *bee* or *feet*

    ea at the beginning or in the middle of a word as in *each* or *meat*

▶ Sort the spelling words under the word with the same /ē/ sound spelling pattern.

m**ea**t

1. neat
2. clean
3. beast
4. deal
5. please
6. easy
7. eat
8. hearing
9. real

b**ee**p Order of answers may vary.

10. keep
11. street
12. seen
13. creek
14. feel
15. tree

UNIT 3 Imagination • **Lesson 2** *The Cat Who Became a Poet*

▶ The /ē/ Sound

Strategies

Visualization Strategy Circle the correct spelling for each word with the /ē/ sound. Write the correct spelling on the line.

16. streat ⟨street⟩ **street** _____

17. ⟨feel⟩ feal **feel** _____

18. ⟨eat⟩ eet **eat** _____

19. easie ⟨easy⟩ **easy** _____

20. ⟨please⟩ pleeze **please** _____

Vowel-Substitution Strategy Substitute the given vowels for the underlined vowel or vowels in each word. Write the new word on the line.

21. s<u>u</u>n (ee) **seen** _____

22. tr<u>ay</u> (ee) **tree** _____

23. r<u>ai</u>l (ea) **real** _____

Rhyming Strategy Write the spelling words that rhyme with the given words and have the same /ē/ sound spelling pattern.

24. beat **neat** _____ **eat** _____

25. feast **beast** _____

26. lean **clean** _____

27. beep **keep** _____

> **Exceptions**
> The /ē/ sound spelled *ee* comes at the beginning of a few words, such as *eel*.
> The /ē/ sound spelled *ea* comes at the end of a few words, such as *sea*.

SPELLING

UNIT 3 Imagination • **Lesson 3** *A Cloak for the Dreamer*

Prefixes

A *prefix*, like a suffix, is added to a base word and changes the meaning of the word. However, prefixes are added to the *beginning* of a word, not the end of a word.

Prefix	(Meaning)	+ Base Word	= New Word	New Meaning
un-	("not or opposite of")	+ *happy*	= *unhappy*	"not happy"
re-	("again")	+ *try*	= *retry*	"try again"
dis-	("not")	+ *trust*	= *distrust*	"to not trust"
bi-	("every two or twice")	+ *annual*	= *biannual*	"twice a year"
mis-	("wrong, wrongly")	+ *use*	= *misuse*	"use wrongly"
tri-	("three")	+ *angle*	= *triangle*	"three angles"

 **Notice how the vocabulary word *unsure* contains the prefix *un-*.**

1. Circle the base word *sure* in the word *unsure* below:

   un(sure)

2. Knowing that the prefix *un-* means "not" or "opposite of," what does the word *unsure* mean?

   possible answer: not sure of something, the opposite of sure

UNIT 3 Imagination • **Lesson 3** *A Cloak for the Dreamer*

▶**Prefixes**

VOCABULARY

Practice

Remember, prefixes are added to the *beginnings* of words and change the meanings of words. Write words with prefixes that match the meaning clues below. Look on page 58 if you need help with the meanings of the prefixes.

3. not kind   **unkind**

4. act again   **react**

5. to not trust   **distrust**

6. draw again   **redraw**

7. the opposite of tie   **untie**

Find the word *unlike* on page 225 of "A Cloak for the Dreamer."

8. Knowing the meaning of the prefix *un-*, what does the word *unlike* mean?

the opposite of like, different

9. The suffix *-ly* could be added to *unlike* to make a word with both a prefix and a suffix. Write the meaning of the new word below:

New Word: unlikely

New Meaning: **not likely, doubtful**

The /ī/ Sound

Word List

1. line
2. pipe
3. wise
4. smile
5. glide
6. high
7. sigh
8. fright
9. sight
10. light

Selection Words

11. fine
12. wide
13. right
14. time
15. night

Pattern Study

The /ī/ sound can be spelled many ways.

i_e with a silent *e* as in *pile*

igh at the end or in the middle of a word as in *sigh* or *sight*

ie at the end of a word as in *tie*

i as in *kind* or *mild*

y at the end of a word as in *by*

Notice the spelling words with the *i_e* and *igh* spellings for the /ī/ sound.

▶ Sort the spelling words under the /ī/ sound spelling pattern. **Order of answers may vary.**

i_e

1. line
2. wise
3. glide
4. pipe
5. smile
6. fine
7. wide
8. time

-igh

9. sigh
10. high

-ight

11. fright
12. sight
13. light
14. right
15. night

UNIT 3 Imagination • **Lesson 3** *A Cloak for the Dreamer*

▶ **The /ī/ Sound**

Strategies

Rhyming Strategy Write the spelling words that rhyme with the given words and have the same /ī/ sound spelling pattern.

16. fight   __fright__   __sight__   __light__

__right__   __night__

17. mine   __line__   __fine__

18. wipe   __pipe__

19. lime   __time__

Meaning Strategy Write the spelling word next to its meaning clue.

20. smart   __wise__

21. the opposite of a frown   __smile__

22. the ability to see   __sight__

Visualization Strategy Look at each word below. If the word is spelled correctly, write the word *correct* on the line. If the word is misspelled, write the correct spelling on the line.

23. high   __correct__

24. ryte   __right__

25. glied   __glide__

26. nite   __night__

Multiple Meanings

Some words have the same spelling and sound but have more than one meaning.

Example: *fly*   *fly*

Spelling: the same

Sound: the same

Meaning: "an insect"   "go through the air"

The context clues within a sentence can help you know the meaning of the word in the sentence.

Example: She swatted at the *fly*. ("an insect")
             Airplanes *fly* in the air. ("go through the air")

 **The vocabulary word *painting* on page 241 of "Picasso" can have two meanings. Order of answers may vary.**

1. Write the two meanings for the word *painting* below. Look in a dictionary if you are unsure.

   painting: **something painted, a picture**

   painting: **the act or art of using paints**

2. Write two sentences: one using *painting* with the first meaning, and one using *painting* with the second meaning.

   sentence 1: **Answers will vary.**

   sentence 2: _____

UNIT 3 Imagination • **Lesson 4** *Picasso*

▶ **Multiple Meanings**

Practice

Match each word from the box next to its meaning clue. Each word will be used twice.

| bat   bill   gum   painting   fan |

3. a small, furry animal that flies   _bat_

4. receipt of money owed   _bill_

5. someone who likes a certain team   _fan_

6. sticky, sweet candy that is chewed   _gum_

7. a machine that blows air   _fan_

8. a bird's beak   _bill_

9. stick used to hit baseballs   _bat_

10. the act of using paints   _painting_

11. a painted picture   _painting_

12. pink skin around your teeth   _gum_

Find the word *right* on page 241 of "Picasso."

13. What does the word *right* mean in the sentence? **the direction opposite of left, the right side of the page**

14. What is another meaning of the word *right?*

Answers may vary: correct, good, proper

VOCABULARY

The /ō/ Sound

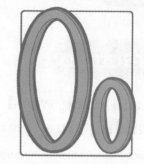

Word List

1. cone
2. vote
3. spoke
4. froze
5. chose
6. coal
7. goal
8. soap
9. choke
10. goat

Selection Words

11. over
12. alone
13. noses
14. most
15. old

Pattern Study

The /ō/ sound can be spelled many ways.

o at the beginning, middle, and end of a word as in *open*, *told*, and *so*

o_e with a silent *e* as in *bone*

oa at the beginning or in the middle of a word as in *oat* or *goal*

_oe at the end of a word as in *toe*

_ow at the end of a word as in *row*

▶ Sort the spelling words under the /ō/ sound spelling pattern. **Order of answers may vary.**

o_e

1. cone
2. spoke
3. chose
4. alone
5. vote
6. froze
7. choke
8. noses

o

9. over
10. most
11. old

oa

12. coal
13. soap
14. goal
15. goat

UNIT 3 Imagination • **Lesson 4** *Picasso*

▶ **The /ō/ Sound**

Strategies

Visualization Strategy Look at each pair of words below. Circle the word with the correct spelling. Write the correct spelling on the line.

16. (cone)   coan   **cone**

17. olde   (old)   **old**

18. (alone)   alown   **alone**

19. (goal)   gole   **goal**

20. voat   (vote)   **vote**

Consonant-Substitution Strategy Substitute the given consonant for the underlined consonant to create a new word. Write the new word on the line.

21. <u>v</u>ote   (n)   **note**

22. <u>g</u>oat   (b)   **boat**

23. <u>n</u>oses   (r)   **roses**

Meaning Strategy Write the spelling word that makes sense in each sentence.

24. Hunting dogs smell scents with their **noses**.

25. One type of natural fuel is **coal**.

26. A raft can be used to cross **over** a river.

27. Wash your hands with **soap** and water.

> **Exception**
> The spelling pattern *o_e* does not always make the /ō/ sound. *come, some, dove, love, move*

SPELLING

Shades of Meaning

When you think of the volume on a radio, you might think of a range of sounds from soft to loud. Shades of meaning for words means that words can have a range of meanings, as on a scale from 1 to 10.

Example:

annoyed > upset > frustrated > mad > angry > furious

Can you tell how each word gets stronger in meaning as it goes up the range?

 **The vocabulary word *extraordinary* on page 257 of "The Emperor's New Clothes" has a specific shade of meaning.**

1. Write the meaning for *extraordinary* as it relates to the courage shown by the king.

   amazing, neat, great

2. Fill in the meaning range with *extraordinary*.

   Range:
   interesting > neat > special > amazing > **extraordinary**

3. Does the word *extraordinary* have a strong shade

   of meaning compared to the other words? **yes**

UNIT 3 Imagination • **Lesson 5** *The Emperor's New Clothes*

▶ **Shades of Meaning**

VOCABULARY

Practice

Remember, shades of meaning has to do with how words fit in a related range of words. Thinking of words that can be a part of a range of meanings can help you learn the meaning of a certain word. Find the word *magnificent* on page 255 of "The Emperor's New Clothes." Use the words from the box to fill in the meaning range below.

great	plain	neat	magnificent

4. <u>plain</u> > <u>neat</u> > <u>great</u> > <u>magnificent</u>

5. Which word has a stronger meaning, *magnificent* or *neat?* <u>magnificent</u>

Complete the shades of meaning ranges below with your own words. **Answers will vary.**

6. whisper > speak > <u>shout</u> > <u>scream</u>

7. tap > touch > <u>hit</u> > <u>pound</u>

8. small > <u>little</u> > <u>tiny</u> > microscopic

The /ō ō/ and /ū/ Sounds

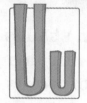

Word List

1. moon
2. cute
3. loose
4. scoop
5. choose
6. dune
7. flute
8. chew
9. few
10. grew

Selection Words

11. new
12. noon
13. rule
14. fool
15. looms

Pattern Study

The /ōō/ sound can be spelled:
oo in the middle of a word as in *loop*
u_e with a silent *e* as in *tune*
ew at the end of a word as in *dew*
_ue at the end of a word as in *due*

The /ū/ sound can be spelled:
u_e with a silent *e* as in *cute*
ew at the end of a word as in *few*
ue at the end of a word as in *tissue*
u at the beginning of a word as in *unit*

▶ Sort the spelling words under the spelling pattern.

/ōō/ spelled *oo*

1. __moon__   4. __looms__   6. __choose__

2. __scoop__   5. __loose__   7. __fool__

3. __noon__   **Order of answers may vary.**

/ōō/ spelled *ew*

8. __grew__   9. __chew__   10. __new__

/ū/ spelled *u_e*   /ū/ spelled *ew*

11. __cute__   12. __few__

UNIT 3 Imagination • **Lesson 5** *The Emperor's New Clothes*

▶ **The /o͞o/ and /u̅/ Sounds**

Strategies

Rhyming Strategy Write the spelling words that rhyme with the given words and have the same spelling pattern.

13. soon   **moon**   **noon**

14. dew   **chew**   **grew**   **new**

15. mute   **cute**

Visualization Strategy Look at each pair of words below. Circle the word with the correct spelling. Write the correct spelling on the line.

16. (grew)   groo   **grew**

17. doone   (dune)   **dune**

18. fule   (fool)   **fool**

Proofreading Strategy Read the sentences carefully and look for misspelled words. Cross out the five misspelled words and write the correct spelling above the word.

It was ~~newn,~~ **noon** and Teresa was hungry for a ~~seupe~~ **scoop** of ice cream. She and her friend rode their ~~noo~~ **new** bikes to the ice cream parlor a ~~fue~~ **few** blocks away. At the store, Teresa and her friend got to ~~chewse~~ **choose** the flavors they wanted.

> **Exceptions:**
> The /o͞o/ sound spelled *oo* is found at the end of some words such as *zoo*, *moo*, and *too*, and at the beginning of a few words such as *ooze*. The words *loose* and *choose* contain the /o͞o/ sound spelled *oo* with a silent *e*.

SPELLING

UNIT 3 Imagination • **Lesson 6** *Roxaboxen*

Unit 3 Review

Remember, suffixes are added to the *ends* of words and change the meanings of words. The suffixes *-er* and *-est* show comparisons, as in the word *whitest* from page 262 of "Roxaboxen."

Think of the base word *white:*

The suffix *-er* means "more." *white + er = whiter* "more white"

The suffix *-est* means "most." *white + est = whitest* "most white"

 **Try It!** **Add the suffix *-er* or *-est* to each word below. Then write the new words on the lines.**

	Suffix	New Word	New Meaning
1. bright	-er	brighter	more bright
2. sweet	-est	sweetest	most sweet
3. light	-est	lightest	most light
4. neat	-er	neater	more neat
5. clean	-est	cleanest	most clean

Complete each sentence using the given word.

6. stronger A rope Sentences will vary.

7. nicest A smile _____

8. gentlest A baby _____

UNIT 3 Imagination • **Lesson 6** *Roxaboxen*

▶ **Unit 3 Review**

VOCABULARY

Practice

Remember, a prefix is a part added to a base word that changes the meaning of the word. Prefixes are added to the *beginning* of a word, not the end of a word.

Prefix	(Meaning)	+ Base Word	= New Word
un-	("not or opposite of")	+ *happy*	= *unhappy* "not happy"
re-	("again")	+ *try*	= *retry* "try again"
dis-	("not")	+ *trust*	= *distrust* "to not trust"
bi-	("every two or twice")	+ *annual*	= *biannual* "twice a year"
mis-	("wrong, wrongly")	+ *use*	= *misuse* "use wrongly"

Notice how the vocabulary word *uncomfortable*, on page 264 of "Roxaboxen," contains the prefix *un-*.

9. Circle the base word *comfort* in the word *uncomfortable* below:

un(comfort)able

10. Knowing that *un-* means "not" or "opposite of," what does *uncomfortable* mean?

not comfortable

Add the prefix *re-*, meaning "again," to the base words below and write the new meanings.

11. *write*   **rewrite**   **to write again**

12. *act*   **react**   **to act again**

13. *charge*   **recharge**   **to charge again**

Answers may vary.

UNIT 3 Imagination • **Lesson 6** *Roxaboxen*

Unit 3 Review

Word List

1. made
2. note
3. sail
4. boat
5. use
6. soon
7. bright
8. pool
9. open
10. each

Selection Words

11. became
12. like
13. reach
14. stone
15. jewels

Pattern Study

Long vowels sound like letter names.
The /ā/ sound can be spelled *a*, *a_e*, *ai*, and *ay*.
The /ē/ sound can be spelled *e*, *e_e*, *ea*, *ee*, and *y*.
The /ī/ sound can be spelled *i_e*, *igh*, *ie*, and *y*.
The /ō/ sound can be spelled *o*, *o_e*, *oe*, and *ow*.
The /ū/ sound can be spelled *u_e*, *ew*, *ue*, and *u*.
The /o͞o/ sound can be spelled *oo*, *u_e*, *ew*, and *ue*.

▶ Sort the spelling words beside the words with the same long-vowel sound. One word will be used twice. **Order of answers may vary.**

meet   1. **each**   2. **reach**   3. **became**

late   4. **sail**   5. **became**   6. **made**

sign   7. **bright**   8. **like**

soap   9. **note**   11. **open**

10. **boat**   12. **stone**

music 13. **use**

boot   14. **soon**   15. **pool**   16. **jewels**

UNIT 3 Imagination • **Lesson 6** *Roxaboxen*

▶ **Unit 3 Review**

Strategies

Visualization Strategy Look at each word below. If the word is spelled correctly, write the word *correct* on the line. If the word is misspelled, write the correct spelling on the line.

17. mayd   made

18. bright   correct

19. stoan   stone

Rhyming Strategy Write the spelling words that rhyme with the given words and have the same long vowel spelling pattern.

20. bail   sail

21. wrote   note

22. moon   soon

23. beach   each, reach

Meaning Strategy Write the spelling word next to its meaning clue.

24. a place for swimming   pool

25. the opposite of closed   open

26. diamonds, rubies, emeralds   jewels

27. grab for something   reach

SPELLING

Name _____ Date _____

Base Word Families

Remember, a **base word** is a word that can have prefixes, suffixes, and endings added to it. Words in the same **base word family** are the different forms of that base word.

Base Word	**Base Word Family Words**	
happy	<u>un</u>happy	happi<u>ly</u>
	happi<u>ness</u>	happi<u>er</u>

 **Try It!** **Notice the Vocabulary Skill Word *weaver* on page 19 of "A New Coat for Anna."**

1. Circle the base word *weave* in the word *weaver* below:
   (weave)r

2. What does the base word *weave* mean in "A New Coat for Anna"?
   possible answer: to make yarn into cloth by overlapping the yarn in a pattern

3. The suffix *-er* is added to the word *weave*. What is a *weaver?*
   possible answer: a person who weaves

4. Then what does the suffix *-er* mean in *weave?*
   possible answer: someone who does a job

Note: The suffix *-er* means "one who" when added to a noun or verb. It can mean "more," as in the word *kinder,* when added to an adjective.

▶ **Base Word Families**

Practice

Remember, words in the same base word family have related meanings to one base word. The groups of words below are all in the same base word family. Underline the base word in each word. Write the base word of each group on the line provided.

Base Word

5. planner	planned	planning	**plan**
6. slippery	slipped	slippers	**slip**
7. unbutton	buttoned	buttoning	**button**
8. safely	unsafe	safety	**safe**
9. harmful	unharmed	harmless	**harm**
10. unfriendly	friendless	friendliness	**friend**
11. action	react	actor	**act**
12. tricolor	colorful	colorless	**color**
13. cheery	cheerful	cheering	**cheer**
14. rewrite	written	writing	**write**

VOCABULARY

Double Consonants

Word List

1. better
2. letter
3. potter
4. rubber
5. soccer
6. ladder
7. hammer
8. scatter
9. dinner
10. slippers

Selection Words

11. tomorrow
12. summer
13. pretty
14. button
15. happy

Pattern Study

Most double consonants are found in the middle or at the end of a word. In this lesson, look for double consonants in words that have a short-vowel sound and end in *-er, -on,* or *-y,* as in *letter, lesson,* and *silly.*

▶ Sort the spelling words under the correct heading.
order of answers may vary
Ends with a double consonant and *-er*

1. better
2. potter
3. soccer
4. letter
5. rubber
6. ladder
7. hammer
8. scatter
9. dinner
10. slippers
11. summer

Ends with a double consonant and *-y*

12. pretty
13. happy

Ends with a double consonant and *-on*

14. button

Ends with a double consonant and *-ow*

15. tomorrow

UNIT 4 Money • **Lesson 1** *A New Coat for Anna*

▶ **Double Consonants**

SPELLING

Strategies

Consonant-Substitution Strategy Substitute the given consonants for the underlined consonants in each word. Write the new word on the line.

16. <u>w</u>etter   (b)   **better**

17. <u>s</u>adder   (l)   **ladder**

18. <u>bl</u>ubber   (r)   **rubber**

Visualization Strategy Circle the correct spelling for each word with a double consonant. Write the correct spelling on the line.

19. (dinner)   dinnar   **dinner**

20. prety   (pretty)   **pretty**

21. (tomorrow)   tommorrow   **tomorrow**

22. leter   (letter)   **letter**

23. socker   (soccer)   **soccer**

Rhyming Strategy Write the spelling word next to its rhyming word below.

24. hotter   **potter**

25. winner   **dinner**

Spelling and Vocabulary Skills • *Double Consonants*   UNIT 4 • Lesson 1   **77**

UNIT 4 Money • **Lesson 2** *Alexander, Who Used to be Rich Last Sunday*

The Suffix -*ly*

Remember, the suffix **-*ly*** can be added to the end of an adjective and change the meaning of the word.

Base Word + Suffix (Meaning) = New Word New Meaning
safe + -ly ("in a ___ way") = safely "in a <u>safe</u> way"

Adding some suffixes, such as **-*ly*,** to words changes the spelling of base words that end in the letter *y*. If a base word ends in *y*, change the *y* to *i* before adding **-*ly*.**
happ<u>y</u> + -ly = happ<u>i</u>ly (the *y* changed to an *i*)

 **Notice the word *positively* on page 29 of "Alexander, Who Used to be Rich Last Sunday."**

1. Circle the base word *positive* in the word below:
(positive)ly

2. Knowing the meaning of the suffix -*ly*, what does the word *positively*
mean? **possible answer: in a positive way**

3. Did the spelling of the word *positive* change or stay the same when
the suffix -*ly* was added? **stayed the same**

4. Add -*ly* to the words below. Change the *y* to *i* if necessary.

	New Word	New Meaning
near	**nearly**	**in a near way**
lucky	**luckily**	**in a lucky way**

▶ **The Suffix -*ly***

Practice

Look at the suffixes that can be added to the words below. Add the suffix, then write the new word, and the meaning of the word with the suffix. Look back to page 54 if you need help with the meanings of the suffixes.

new meaning
answers may vary

Base Word		New Word	New Meaning
Example:			
happy	-ness	happiness	"state of being happy"
5. bright	-ly	brightly	in a bright way
6. rich	-ly	richly	in a rich way
7. fear	-ful	fearful	full of fear
8. sweet	-ly	sweetly	in a sweet way
9. play	-ful	playful	full of play

Find the word *friendly* on page 33 of "Alexander, Who Used to be Rich Last Sunday."

10. Knowing the meaning of the suffix -*ly*, what does the word *friendly* mean? in the manner of a friend

11. When Alexander brought bottles to "Friendly's Market," he said the people there were not friendly. What is a prefix you could add to the word *friendly* to mean "not friendly"?

prefix: un- new word: unfriendly

VOCABULARY

Final Double Consonants

Word List

1. spill
2. hill
3. gull
4. smell
5. mess
6. odd
7. add
8. cliff
9. mitt
10. fuzz

Selection Words

11. all
12. still
13. fall
14. till
15. guess

Pattern Study

Most double consonants are found in the middle or at the end of a word. This lesson focuses on words that have a short-vowel sound and end in a double consonant, such as *will* and *less*. The double consonants *ll*, *ss*, *dd*, *ff*, *tt*, and *zz* are often found at the end of words.

▶ Sort the spelling words under the correct heading.

order of answers may vary

Ends with *ll*

1. spill
2. gull
3. smell
4. hill
5. all
6. still
7. fall
8. till

Ends with *dd*

9. odd
10. add

Ends with *ss*

11. mess
12. guess

Ends with *tt*

13. mitt

Ends with *zz*

14. fuzz

Ends with *ff*

15. cliff

▶ **Final Double Consonants**

Strategies

 Rhyming Strategy Write the spelling words that rhyme with the given words.

16. buzz   fuzz

17. will   spill   hill   still   till

18. wall   fall   all

19. less   mess   guess

20. dull   gull

 Visualization Strategy Circle the correct spelling for each word. Write the correct spelling on the line.

21. spil   (spill)   spill

22.(guess)   gess   guess

23. mes   (mess)   mess

24.(mitt)   mit   mitt

25. od   (odd)   odd

 Meaning Strategy Write the spelling word that makes sense in each sentence.

26. The scent of roses is a sweet ___smell___.

27. The best view of the city is from that ___cliff___.

SPELLING

UNIT 4 Money • **Lesson 3** *Kids Did It! in Business*

Business and Technology Words

As business and technology changes, so does our language.

Remember, a **context clue** is information within a sentence or nearby sentences that helps identify the meaning of a word.

He installed a new <u>software</u> program into his computer.

Unfamiliar word: *software*
Clue Words in the text: *installed, program, computer*
Meaning: *Software* is a type of *program installed* into a *computer*.

Related Words: *computer, hardware*

 **Read the sentence on page 40 of "Kids Did It! in Business" that contains the word *profitable*.**

1. What are some context clues for the meaning of *profitable?*

   possible clue words: selling, business

2. What is the base word of the word *profitable?* **profit**

3. What are some related words? **money, earnings, sales**

4. What is the definition for *profitable* in the dictionary?

   giving a profit, potential money gained

UNIT 4 Money • **Lesson 3** *Kids Did It! in Business*

▶ **Business and Technology Words**

Practice

Find the word *merchandise* on page 40 of "Kids Did It! in Business" and think through how context clues, related words, and a dictionary can help you discover its meaning.

Read the sentence that contains the word *merchandise*.

5. What are some context clues within the surrounding sentences that can help you understand the meaning of *merchandise*?

   possible clue words: order, pins, scarves

6. Look in a dictionary to find the base word of the word *merchandise*.

   Base Word: **merchant**

   What is a merchant? **one who sells goods for a profit**

7. What are some words related to the word *merchandise*?

   sales, goods, things

8. What is the definition for *merchandise* in the dictionary?

   things for sale, goods

9. Knowing the meaning of *merchandise*, what is Ebony Hood's job title? **a merchant**

VOCABULARY

UNIT 4 Money • **Lesson 3** *Kids Did It! in Business*

Contractions

Word List

1. he'll
2. she'll
3. we'll
4. I'd
5. we'd
6. they'll
7. you'd
8. that's
9. she'd
10. you'll

Selection Words

11. it's
12. she's
13. what's
14. I'm
15. can't

Pattern Study

A **contraction** is a word formed from two or more words. Some letters are left out when the two words combine. An apostrophe (') marks the spot where the letters were dropped. Some contractions look the same, but mean two different things. For example, *he'd* means "he had" and "he would." Only one contraction, *I'm*, is made with the word *am*. Only one contraction, *let's*, is made with the word *us*.

▶ Sort the spelling words under the word that is part of the contraction. **order of answers may vary**

will, shall	would, had	is, has
1. he'll	6. I'd	10. that's
2. she'll	7. we'd	11. it's
3. we'll	8. you'd	12. what's
4. they'll	9. she'd	13. she's
5. you'll		

not	am
14. can't	15. I'm

▶ Contractions

SPELLING

Strategies

 Meaning Strategy **Write the spelling word that could replace the underlined words in each sentence.**

16. Teresa and I have decided <u>we would</u> **we'd** like to go sledding.

17. Since <u>it is</u> **it's** cold outside, <u>we will</u> **we'll** have to put on warm coats.

18. We are going to call some friends to see if <u>they will</u> **they'll** come over too.

19. There is lots of snow on the ground, so <u>it is</u> **it's** going to be a fun day.

 Meaning Strategy **Write the words that combine to make each contraction. Some contractions can be made by two sets of words.**

20. she'll **she** + **will**

21. I'd **I** + **had**
    and **I** + **would**

22. you'll **you** + **will**

23. we'd **we** + **had**
    and **we** + **would**

Exceptions
One contraction changes the spelling and the sound of the original word. *will + not = won't* (not *willn't*)

The Endings -ed and -ing

When the endings **-ed** and **-ing** are added to a base word, the meaning of the base word changes.
   The **-ed** ending shows an action that has already happened in the *past*.
   The **-ing** ending shows an action that is happening now.

play + -ed = play<u>ed</u>   The children <u>played</u> yesterday.
play + -ing = play<u>ing</u> The children are <u>playing</u> now.

Notice how adding the endings **-ed** and **-ing** to some base words changes the spelling of the words.

   stud<u>y</u>, stud<u>i</u>ed   bit<u>e</u>, biting   hit, hit<u>t</u>ing

 **Try It!** **Notice how the word *glared* on page 52 of "The Cobbler's Song" has the -ed ending.**

1. Circle *glare*, meaning "to give an angry look," in the word below:
ⓖⓛⓐⓡⓔd

2. Knowing how the ending *-ed* changes the meaning of a word, what
does the word *glared* mean? **gave an angry look in the**
past, looked in an angry way

3. How would you spell the word formed by *glare + ing?* **glaring**

4. Write sentences for the two words that show their meanings.
glared: **answers will vary**

glaring: _____

UNIT 4 Money • **Lesson 4** *The Cobbler's Song*

► **The Endings -ed and -ing**

Practice

Remember, the endings *-ed* and *-ing* change the meanings of words.

The *-ed* ending shows an action that has happened in the *past*.

The *-ing* ending shows an action that is happening now.

The word *recognizing* on page 49 of "The Cobbler's Song" has the *-ing* ending.

5. Circle the base word *recognize*, meaning "to know and remember from before," in the word below:

recognizing

6. Knowing how the ending *-ing* changes the meaning of a word, what does the word *recognizing* mean? **possible answer:**
knowing or remembering from before

7. How did the spelling of the word *recognize* change when the ending *-ing* was added? **the silent *e* was dropped**

8. How would you spell the word formed by *recognize* + *-ed?*
recognized

9. Write sentences for the two words that show you know their meanings.

recognizing: **answers will vary**

recognized: _____

VOCABULARY

UNIT 4 Money • **Lesson 4** *The Cobbler's Song*

Adding -ed and -ing

Word List

1. making
2. biting
3. diving
4. hiking
5. skated
6. prized
7. shaking
8. skating
9. hiding
10. shining

Selection Words

11. thinking
12. entered
13. opened
14. passing
15. safekeeping

Pattern Study

For words with a **short vowel-consonant** pattern, double the final consonant before adding **-ed** or **-ing**.   clap, cla**pp**ed, cla**pp**ing

For words with a silent *e*, drop the *e* before adding the **-ed** or **-ing**.   skate, skat**ed**, skat**ing**

For words ending in *consonant-y*, change the *y* to *i* before adding **-ed**.   stud**y**, stud**ied**, stud**ying**

▶ Sort the spelling words under the correct heading.

order of answers may vary

Words with the *-ing* ending

1. making
2. biting
3. diving
4. hiking
5. shaking
6. skating
7. hiding
8. shining
9. thinking
10. passing
11. safekeeping

Words with the *-ed* ending

12. skated
13. prized
14. entered
15. opened

UNIT 4 Money • **Lesson 4** *The Cobbler's Song*

▶ **Adding -ed and -ing**

Strategies

Visualization Strategy Circle the correct spelling for each word with the *-ed* or *-ing* ending. Write the correct spelling on the line.

16. prizd (prized) **prized**

17. (shining) shineing **shining**

18. (hiding) hidding **hiding**

19. thinkeing (thinking) **thinking**

Rhyming Strategy Write the spelling words that rhyme with the given words.

20. biking **hiking**

21. rated **skated**

22. blinking **thinking**

23. waking **making**   **shaking**

Meaning Strategy Write the spelling word next to its meaning clue.

24. came in the room **entered**

25. the opposite of closed **opened**

26. using the teeth to chew **biting**

27. climbing a mountain **hiking**

Exceptions

When the ending *-ing* is added to the word *ski*, the *i* is not dropped. The new word is *skiing*.

Spelling and Vocabulary Skills • *Adding* -ed *and* -ing   UNIT 4 • Lesson 4   **89**

SPELLING

UNIT 4 Money • **Lesson 5** *Four Dollars and Fifty Cents*

Compound Words

> A **compound word** is a single word formed from two words.
>
> bird + house = birdhouse   "a *house* for a *bird*"
>
> A compound word can have the same meaning as the two words in it, as in *birdhouse*, or it can have a new meaning.
>
> cow + boy = cowboy   "a male who herds cattle"
> (not a *boy* that is a *cow*)

 **Read the sentence with the word *buckboard* on page 59 of "Four Dollars and Fifty Cents."**

1. Separate the compound word *buckboard* into its two words:

   buckboard = **buck** _____ + **board** _____

2. If the horses are hitched, meaning "tied up," to a buckboard, then what do you think the compound word *buckboard* means?

   a board for hitching or tying up horses

3. The word *board* means "a flat piece of wood." Look in a dictionary to

   find out what the word *buck* means. **possible answer: a**

   male deer, to jump with an arched back

4. The compound word *buckboard* means "a kind of open wagon." Does it have the exact same meaning as the two words that form it?

   no

▶ **Compound Words**

VOCABULARY

Practice

Create a compound word from the two given words. Fill in the blanks to define the new compound words.

head + ache = headache "an *ache* in the *head* "

5. head + band = **headband** "a **band** _____ worn on the **head** "

6. sun + shine = **sunshine** "the **shine** _____ of a bright **sun** "

7. gold + fish = **goldfish** "a **gold** _____-colored **fish** "

Find the word *rawhide* on page 63 of "Four Dollars and Fifty Cents."

8. Look up the definition for the word *raw* as it relates to *hide*.

raw: **having the skin rubbed off** _____

hide: the skin of an animal used to make leather

9. What do you think the word *rawhide* means in the sentence?
possible answer: leather made from rubbed animal skin

10. Look up *rawhide* in a dictionary. Does it match the meaning you wrote above? **yes** _____

UNIT 4 Money • **Lesson 5** *Four Dollars and Fifty Cents*

Adding *-s* or *-es* to Make Plurals

Word List

1. berries
2. bunnies
3. guppies
4. hobbies
5. pennies
6. puppies
7. ponies
8. babies
9. donkeys
10. families

Selection Words

11. dollars
12. horses
13. sleeves
14. cowboys
15. britches

Pattern Study

To make words **plural,** meaning "more than one," add the ending *-s* or *-es.* The letter *s* is added to most words to make them plural.

dog + s = dog<u>s</u>

The letters *es* are added to words that end in *ch, sh, s, ss, x, z,* or *zz.*

bo<u>x</u> + es = bo<u>xes</u>

When a word ends in a *consonant-y,* change the *y* to *i,* and then add *-es.*

fl<u>y</u> + es = fl<u>ies</u>

If a word ends in *vowel-y,* just add *-s.*

t<u>oy</u> + s = toy<u>s</u>

If a word ends in silent *e,* just add *-s.*

cak<u>e</u> + s = cake<u>s</u> (not cak<u>ees</u>)

▶ Sort the spelling words under the correct heading.

Changed *y* to *i* and added *-es*

1. berries   4. hobbies   7. ponies
2. bunnies   5. pennies   8. babies
3. guppies   6. puppies   9. families

order of answers may vary

Added *-s*

10. donkeys   12. horses   14. cowboys
11. dollars   13. sleeves

▶**Adding -s or -es**

SPELLING

Strategies

Rhyming Strategy Write the spelling word next to its rhyming word below.

15. collars **dollars**   18. leaves **sleeves**

16. stitches **britches**   19. lobbies **hobbies**

17. ferries **berries**

Meaning Strategy Write the spelling word that matches the meaning clue.

20. baby rabbits **bunnies**   23. the arms of a shirt **sleeves**

21. infants **babies**   24. small fish **guppies**

22. mom, dad, kids **families**

Visualization Strategy Circle the correct spelling for each word. Write the correct spelling on the line.

25. babys (babies)   **babies**

26. cowboies (cowboys)   **cowboys**

27. (dollars) dollares   **dollars**

28. berrys (berries)   **berries**

29. horsees (horses)   **horses**

Exceptions
Some words, such as *britches* or *pants*, are always plural and have no singular form.

UNIT 4 Money • **Lesson 6** *The Go-Around Dollar*

Money Words

Some words relate to money. Learning the meanings of those words can be easy if you:

1. Look for context clues.
2. Think about the meaning of the base word.
3. Check in a dictionary to find the definition.

Remember, a context clue is information within a sentence or nearby sentences that helps identify the meaning of a word.

   The woman got back <u>change</u> for her fifty-dollar bill when she bought the sweater.

Money word: *change*
Clue Words: *got, fifty-dollar, bill, bought*
Related Words: *cash, coins*
Meaning: *change* is something *given back* when you make a purchase with *dollars*

Read the sentence on page 73 of "The Go-Around Dollar" that contains the Vocabulary Skill Word *circulation*.

1. What are some context clues for the meaning of *circulation?*

   go into, all over, to be used, other places

2. What is the definition for *circulation* in the dictionary?

   movement around many different places

UNIT 4 Money • **Lesson 6** *The Go-Around Dollar*

▶ Money Words

Practice

Find the word *formula* on page 80 of "The Go-Around Dollar" and think through how you can apply context clues, related words, and a dictionary to discover its meaning.

Read the sentence that contains the word *formula*.

3. What are some context clues within the sentences that can help you understand the meaning of *formula?*

possible clue words: secret, inks, used to print

4. Circle the base word *form* in the word *formula*.

(form)ula

5. The base word *form* means "to make or shape." What is the definition for *formula* in the dictionary?

an explanation for how to make something

6. Knowing the meaning of *formula*, notice that the synonyms below could replace the word *formula* in the sentence.

"The *formula* for the black and green inks . . ."
"The *recipe* for the black and green inks . . ."
"The *mixture* for the black and green inks . . ."
"The *ingredients* for the black and green inks . . ."

VOCABULARY

Compound Words

Word List

1. playground
2. underground
3. chalkboard
4. cardboard
5. spacewalk
6. sidewalk
7. rainbow
8. anything
9. campfire
10. eyelash

Selection Words

11. shoelaces
12. something
13. overprinting
14. neighborhood
15. sometimes

Pattern Study

Remember, a compound word is a word made of two words joined together.

bird + house = birdhouse

It is easy to spell a compound word if you know how to spell each of the two words that form it.

side + walk = sidewalk
play + ground = playground
ear + ring = earring

▶ Sort the spelling words under their common endings. **order of answers may vary**

-ground

1. **playground**
2. **underground**

-board

3. **chalkboard**
4. **cardboard**

-bow

5. **rainbow**

-walk

6. **sidewalk**
7. **spacewalk**

-thing

8. **anything**
9. **something**

-times

10. **sometimes**

UNIT 4 Money • **Lesson 6** *The Go-Around Dollar*

▶ **Compound Words**

Strategies

Visualization Strategy Circle the correct spelling for each word. Write the correct spelling on the line.

11. cardbard (cardboard) — **cardboard**

12. (spacewalk) spasewalk — **spacewalk**

13. eylash (eyelash) — **eyelash**

14. (overprinting) ovrprinting — **overprinting**

15. naborhood (neighborhood) — **neighborhood**

Compound Word Strategy Write the two words that make each compound word.

16. anything   **any** + **thing**

17. underground   **under** + **ground**

18. chalkboard   **chalk** + **board**

19. eyelash   **eye** + **lash**

Meaning Strategy Write the compound word that matches the meaning clue.

20. printing something too many times   **overprinting**

21. a fire you make when camping   **campfire**

22. laces for tying shoes   **shoelaces**

SPELLING

UNIT 4   Money • **Lesson 7** *Uncle Jed's Barbershop*

Unit 4 Review

> Remember, when the endings **-ed** and **-ing** are added
> to a base word, the meaning of the base word changes.
>   The **-ed** ending shows an action in the past.
>   The **-ing** ending shows an action in the present.
>
> play + -ed = play<u>ed</u>   The children <u>played</u> yesterday.
> play + -ing = play<u>ing</u>   The children are <u>playing</u> now.
>
> Remember how adding the endings **-ed** and **-ing** to
> some base words changes the spelling of the words.

 **The word *failing* on page 100 of "Uncle Jed's Barbershop" has the *-ing* ending.**

1. Circle *fail*, meaning "to not succeed, lose," in the word below:
   (fail)ing

2. Knowing how the ending *-ing* changes the meaning of a word, what

   does the word *failing* mean? __**not succeeding, losing**__

3. Did the spelling of *fail* change when *-ing* was added? __**no**____

4. How would you spell the word formed by *fail + ed?* __**failed**____

5. Write sentences for the two words that show their meanings.

   failing: __**answers will vary**_____

   _____

   failed: _____

   _____

▶Unit 4 Review

VOCABULARY

Practice

Remember, the suffix *-ly* can be added to the end of a word and change the meaning of the word.

Base Word + Suffix (Meaning) = New Word New Meaning
safe + -ly ("in a ___ way") = safely "in a <u>safe</u> way"

Remember, if a base word ends in *y*, change the *y* to *i* before adding the *-ly*.

happ<u>y</u> + -ly = happ<u>i</u>ly (the *y* changed to an *i*)

Add the suffix *-ly* to the words below. Change the *y* to *i* when necessary. Write the new words and the new meanings on the lines.

		New Word	New Meaning
6.	dear	dearly	in a dear way
7.	lucky	luckily	in a lucky way
8.	angry	angrily	in an angry way

For each word below, write which suffix was added. Then write the base word of the word and the meaning of the word.

	Example: happiness	-ness	happy	"state of being happy"
9.	tightly	-ly	tight	in a tight way
10.	richly	-ly	rich	in a rich way
11.	playful	-ful	play	full of play
12.	sweetly	-ly	sweet	in a sweet way

UNIT 4 Money • **Lesson 7** *Uncle Jed's Barbershop*

Unit 4 Review

Word List

1. offer
2. winner
3. zipper
4. will
5. well
6. he'd
7. isn't
8. taking
9. monkeys
10. stitches

Selection Words

11. used
12. cutting
13. clippers
14. saving
15. died

Pattern Study

This lesson reviews words with double consonants, words with final double consonants, contractions, how to add **-ed** and **-ing,** how to add **-s** or **-es,** and how to form compound words.

▶ Sort the spelling words under the correct heading.
order of answers may vary

Words with -*ing*

1. **cutting**   2. **saving**   3. **taking**

Words with final double consonants

4. **well**   5. **will**

Words with middle double consonants

6. **offer**   8. **zipper**

7. **winner**   9. **clippers**

Contractions

10. **he'd**   11. **isn't**

Words with -*ed*

12. **used**   13. **died**

UNIT 4 Money • **Lesson 7** *Uncle Jed's Barbershop*

SPELLING

Strategies

Visualization Strategy Circle the correct spelling for each word. Write the correct spelling on the line.

14. (offer)   ofer   **offer** _____

15. monkeies (monkeys) **monkeys** _____

16. takeing   (taking)   **taking** _____

17. cuting   (cutting) **cutting** _____

Rhyming Strategy Write the spelling words that rhyme with the given words.

18. bill   **will** _____   21. flipper **zipper** _____

19. making **taking** _____   22. thinner **winner** _____

20. lied   **died** _____

Meaning Strategy Write the spelling word next to its meaning clue.

23. tools for cutting   **clippers** _____

24. is not   **isn't** _____

25. more than one monkey   **monkeys** _____

26. not sick   **well** _____

27. keeping, not using   **saving** _____

UNIT 5 Storytelling • **Lesson I** *A Story, A Story*

Categories

Remember, you can learn a lot more about a word by separating it into specific categories. A **category** is a group of things that all have some of the same features.

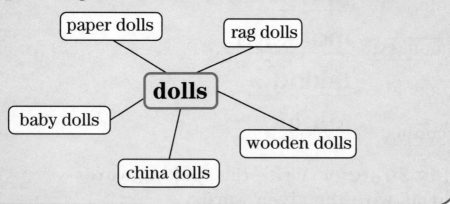

paper dolls

rag dolls

dolls

baby dolls

wooden dolls

china dolls

Try It! **Find the word *gum* on page 112 of "A Story, A Story."**

1. What type of gum is Ananse using in the story?

   latex gum

2. How is the gum described in the story?

   the gum is sticky latex gum

3. Fill in the word map to show two specific types of gum.

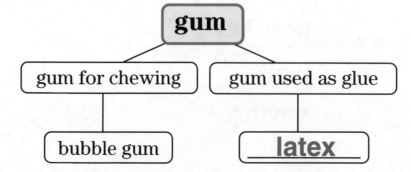

gum

gum for chewing

gum used as glue

bubble gum

latex

UNIT 5 Storytelling • **Lesson I** *A Story, A Story*

▶ **Categories**

Practice

Find the vocabulary word *flamboyant* **on page 112 of "A Story, A Story."**

4. What is the word *flamboyant* describing in the story?

a tree

5. Find *flamboyant* in the dictionary. What does *flamboyant* mean?

possible answers: colorful; wavy; elaborate

6. What is special about the tree, according to the story?

fairies like to dance under that tree

7. Fill in the word map with *flamboyant*.

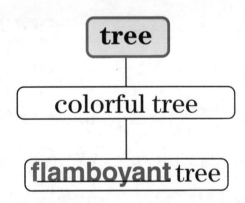

tree

colorful tree

__flamboyant__ tree

VOCABULARY

UNIT 5 Storytelling• **Lesson I** *A Story, A Story*

Consonant Blends

Word List

1. splint
2. splash
3. splatter
4. sprinkle
5. sprout
6. spring
7. strap
8. strike
9. string
10. streak

Selection Words

11. stronger
12. spun
13. stories
14. sticky
15. slap

Pattern Study

Consonant blends are groups of two or three letters in which the sound of each letter can be heard. Blends that begin with the letter *s*, such as the ones below, are called *s*-blends.

spl as in *splash*	**sp** as in *spider*
spr as in *sprout*	**st** as in *stop*
str as in *string*	**sl** as in *slip*

▶ Sort the spelling words with consonant blends under the correct heading.

order of answers may vary

Words with *spl*

1. splint
2. splash
3. splatter

Words with *spr*

4. sprinkle
5. spring
6. sprout

Word with *sp*

7. spun

Words with *str*

8. strap
9. strike
10. string
11. streak
12. stronger

Words with *st*

13. stories
14. sticky

Word with *sl*

15. slap

▶ **Consonant Blends**

Strategies

Visualization Strategy Circle and then write the spelling word that is spelled correctly.

16. splater   (splatter)   **splatter**

17. (sprinkle)   sprinkel   **sprinkle**

18. strik   (strike)   **strike**

19. (spun)   spunn   **spun**

20. stiky   (sticky)   **sticky**

Rhyming Strategy Write the spelling word that rhymes with each word below.

21. map   **strap**   **slap**

22. batter   **splatter**

23. weak   **streak**

order of
answers
may vary

Consonant-Substitution Strategy Substitute the given consonants for the underlined consonants in each word. Write the new word on the line.

24. splash   (t)   **stash**

25. spun   (t)   **stun**

26. slap   (tr)   **strap**

SPELLING

UNIT 5 Storytelling • **Lesson 2** *Oral History*

Homographs

> **Homographs** are words that have the same spelling, but have different pronunciations and meanings.
>
> **Example:** *live* and *live* are homographs
>
> | | |
> |---|---|
> | *live* (liv) | "to make one's home" |
> | *live* (līv) | "living" |
>
> Knowing the meanings of homographs and how to pronounce them helps you know the context in which the word is being used.

 **Read the sentence containing the word *records* from page 120 of "Oral History."**

1. Does the letter *e* in *records* from page 120

make the /e/ sound or the /ē/ sound? __the /e/ sound__

2. What is the meaning of the word *records* in the sentence?

__possible answers: documents, written__
__history, historical journals__

Say *records* with the /ē/ sound, instead of the /e/ sound and the second syllable stressed. (rē-kordz') The words *records* (/e/) and *records* (/ē/) are homographs.

3. Find the definitions for the two words in a dictionary.

records (/e/): __written accounts__

records (/ē/): __to write down__

UNIT 5 Storytelling • **Lesson 2** *Oral History*

Remember, homographs are words that are spelled alike but have different pronunciations and different meanings.

The words *dove* and *dove* are homographs. Notice that they have the same spelling.

4. What is the meaning of the word *dove* in the context of the sentence below?
   The young *dove* had white feathers.

   dove: **a type of bird**

5. Circle how the word *dove* is pronounced in the sentence above.
   (duv)   dōv

6. What is the meaning of the word *dove* in the context of the sentence below?
   The swimmer *dove* into the cold water.

   dove: **jumped headfirst into water**

7. Circle how the word *dove* is pronounced in the sentence above.
   duv   (dōv)

VOCABULARY

UNIT 5 Storytelling • **Lesson 2** *Oral History*

The /n/ and /r/ Sounds

Word List

1. *know*
2. *knee*
3. *kneel*
4. *knife*
5. *knit*
6. *wrap*
7. *wren*
8. *wreck*
9. *wrist*
10. *wrong*

Selection Words

11. *write*
12. *wrinkle*
13. *knew*
14. *known*
15. *written*

Pattern Study

The /r/ and the /n/ sounds are special because they have spellings that involve a silent letter. The blend *kn_* at the beginning of a word makes the /n/ sound. The letter *k* is silent in words such as *know* and *knit*.

The blend *wr_* at the beginning of a word makes the /r/ sound. The letter *w* is silent. Examples of this are the words *written* and *wrap*.

▶ Sort the spelling words with silent letters under the correct heading.

order of answers may vary

/n/ spelled kn_	/r/ spelled wr_
1. know	8. wrap
2. knee	9. wren
3. kneel	10. wreck
4. knife	11. wrist
5. knit	12. wrong
6. knew	13. write
7. known	14. wrinkle
	15. written

UNIT 5 Storytelling • **Lesson 2** *Oral History*

▶ The /n/ and /r/ Sounds

SPELLING

Strategies

Visualization Strategy Circle and then write the spelling word that has a silent *k* or *w*.

16. (write) right **write**   19. rap (wrap) **wrap**

17. new (knew) **knew**   20. (wrinkle) rinkel **wrinkle**

18. no (know) **know**

Rhyming Strategy Write the spelling word that rhymes with each word below.

21. bright **write**   24. fit **knit**

22. mitten **written**   25. trap **wrap**

23. show **know**

Proofreading Strategy Each underlined word is misspelled. Write the correct spelling of the word on the line.

26. Olympic athletes are <u>nown</u> as the best in their sports. **known**

27. Calligraphy is a way to <u>rite</u> letters in a fancy style. **write**

28. The human <u>rist</u> connects the hand to the arm. **wrist**

29. It is <u>rong</u> to not tell the truth. **wrong**

30. A seatbelt can save a life in a car <u>reck</u>. **wreck**

Name _____ Date _____

The Suffixes -*ly* and -*ness*

Remember, the suffixes -**ly** and -**ness** can be added to the ends of words to change the meanings of the words. If a base word ends in *y*, change the *y* to *i* before adding -**ly** or -**ness**.

Base Word + Suffix (Meaning)   = New Word
happy   + -*ly* ("in a way")   = *happily*
        New Meaning   "in a *happy* way"
happy   + -*ness* ("being")   = *happiness*
        New Meaning   "a state of being *happy*"

 **Notice how the word *silliness* on page 133 of "Storm in the Night" has the suffix -*ness*.**

1. Knowing the meaning of the suffix -***ness***, what does the word

silliness mean? **being silly** _____

2. Did the spelling of the base word change when the suffix -***ness***

was added? How? **yes, the *y* changed to an *i*** _____

Notice how the vocabulary word *darkness* on page 139 of "Storm in the Night" also has the suffix -*ness*.

3. What does the word *darkness* mean? **being dark** _____

4. Use the word *darkness* in a sentence that shows the meaning of

darkness. **Answers will vary.** _____

_____

UNIT 5 Storytelling • **Lesson 3** *Storm in the Night*

▶ The Suffixes *-ly* and *-ness*

VOCABULARY

Practice

Remember, suffixes are added to the ends of words and change the meanings of words. Add the given suffixes to the words below. Write the new word and the meaning of the new word on the lines provided. Meanings will vary.

Example:

| *kind* | *-ness* | *kindness* | "state of being *kind*" |
| Word | Suffix | New Word | New Meaning |

5. sweet -ness		sweetness	state of being sweet
6. bright -ly		brightly	in a bright way
7. sad -ly		sadly	in a sad way
8. good -ness		goodness	a state of being good
9. pretty -ness		prettiness	a state of being pretty

Use each of the five new words above in a sentence that shows you know the meaning of each new word.

10. Sentences will vary _____

11. _____

12. _____

13. _____

14. _____

Name _____ Date _____

Words with *lf*, *mb*, and ■tch

Word List

1. batch
2. catch
3. latch
4. match
5. lamb
6. limb
7. comb
8. climb
9. calf
10. thumb
11. ditch
12. crumb

Selection Words

13. scratched
14. kitchen
15. half

Pattern Study

The letter *l* is silent in words that end in **lf**, such as *ca<u>l</u>f* and *ha<u>l</u>f*.

The letter *b* is silent when a word ends in **mb**, as in *la<u>mb</u>*.

Words with short-vowel sounds that end with /ch/ have the /ch/ sound spelled ■**tch**. The *t* is silent in the ■**tch**, as in *ca<u>tch</u>*.

▶ Sort the spelling words under the correct heading.

order of answers may vary

Silent *l* in *lf*

1. calf   2. half

/ch/ spelled ■*tch*

3. batch   7. scratched
4. catch   8. kitchen
5. latch   9. ditch
6. match

Silent *b* in *mb*

10. limb   13. lamb
11. comb   14. thumb
12. climb   15. crumb

▶ **Words with** *lf*, *mb*, **and** ■**tch**

Strategies

Rhyming Strategy Write the spelling words that rhyme with the given words and have the same spelling pattern.

16. stitch __ditch__

17. hatch __batch__ __catch__ __latch__ __match__

18. numb __thumb__ __crumb__

Visualization Strategy Circle the correct spelling for each word with a silent letter. Write the correct spelling on the line.

19. haff (half) __half__

20. (kitchen) kichen __kitchen__

21. (calf) caff __calf__

22. clim (climb) __climb__

23. dich (ditch) __ditch__

Meaning Strategy Match the correct spelling word next to its meaning clue.

24. where food is prepared __kitchen__

25. one of the five fingers __thumb__

26. divided in two __half__

27. starts a fire __match__

> **Exceptions**
> The *l* is not always silent in the *lf* combination, as in *self*. The *b* in *mb* is not silent when it is followed by an *le*, as in *crum__ble__* or *thim__ble__*.

SPELLING

Cultural Words

Culture is the customs and beliefs of a certain group of people. Many words in "Carving the Pole" relate to the Native American culture. Remember, to discover the meaning of an unfamiliar word:
1. Look for context clues.
2. Think of related words or the base word.
3. Check in a dictionary to find the definition.
Remember, a **context clue** is information within the text (a sentence or nearby sentences) that helps identify the meaning of a word.

 **Read the sentence from page 146 of "Carving the Pole" that contains the word *tribe*.**

1. What are some context clues within the sentences that can help you understand the meaning of *tribe*?

possible clue words: group, family, clan

2. What are some related words?

Tsimshian, Northwest Coast Indians, Eagle Clan

3. What is the definition for *tribe* in the dictionary?

a group with the same ancestors, or customs

►**Cultural Words**

Practice

Find the word *reservation* on page 146 of "Carving the Pole" and think about how context clues, related words, the base word, and a dictionary can help you discover its meaning.

Read the sentence that contains the word *reservation*.

4. What are some context clues within the surrounding sentences that can help you understand the meaning of a *reservation?*

possible words: live, Klallam Indians, tribe

5. Notice the base word of the word *reservation*.
Base Word: *reserve*

What does the word *reserve* mean? **to set aside, to save**

6. What is a possible meaning for a place known as a *reservation?*

possible definition: a place set aside for a tribe

7. What is the definition for *reservation* in the dictionary?

land saved for Native Americans by the

government

VOCABULARY

The /ə/ Sound

Word List

1. woman
2. eleven
3. even
4. garden
5. happen
6. bottom
7. cannon
8. dragon
9. horizon
10. lesson

Selection Words

11. totem
12. important
13. legend
14. system
15. listen

Pattern Study

The /ə/ sound is a vowel sound in the unstressed syllable of a word and can be spelled with any vowel. The letters *a*, *o*, or *e* usually spell the /ə/ sound.

The /ə/ sound can be spelled *a* as in *wom**a**n*.
The /ə/ sound can spelled *o* as in *less**o**n*.
The /ə/ sound can be spelled *e* as in *ev**e**n*.

▶ Sort the spelling words under the correct heading.
order of answers may vary

/ə/ spelled *a*	/ə/ spelled *o*	/ə/ spelled *e*
1. woman	3. bottom	8. eleven
2. important	4. cannon	9. even
	5. dragon	10. garden
	6. horizon	11. happen
	7. lesson	12. totem
		13. legend
		14. system
		15. listen

▶ **The /ə/ Sound**

Strategies

Visualization Strategy Circle the correct spelling for each word. Write the correct spelling on the line.

16. (listen) listin <u>**listen**</u>

17. dragun (dragon) <u>**dragon**</u>

18. bottem (bottom) <u>**bottom**</u>

19. (legend) legind <u>**legend**</u>

20. (horizon) horizen <u>**horizon**</u>

Meaning Strategy Write the spelling word next to its meaning clue.

21. a female adult <u>**woman**</u>

22. the number 11 <u>**eleven**</u>

23. where sky meets earth <u>**horizon**</u>

24. a place where flowers grow <u>**garden**</u>

25. to use the ears to hear <u>**listen**</u>

26. a scaly creature <u>**dragon**</u>

27. a carved pole <u>**totem**</u>

28. a myth or story <u>**legend**</u>

29. equal, balanced <u>**even**</u>

SPELLING

UNIT 5 Storytelling • **Lesson 5** *The Keeping Quilt*

Words with Foreign Origins

Many words you use every day come from other languages. In "The Keeping Quilt," many of the words come from foreign languages, such as Hebrew and French. Remember, to discover the meaning of any unfamiliar word:

1. Look for context clues.
2. Think of related words or the base word.
3. Check in a dictionary to find the definition.

Remember, a context clue is information within the text (a sentence or nearby sentences) that helps identify the meaning of a word.

 **Try It!** **Read the sentence from page 161 of "The Keeping Quilt" that contains the word *bouquet*.**

1. What are some context clues within the sentences that can help you understand the meaning of *bouquet?*

possible words: gold, bread, salt

2. The *-et* ending in *bouquet* makes the /ā/ sound and is a French spelling pattern. Look in a dictionary to find the definition of the word *bouquet*.

definition: **a bunch or grouping of flowers**

3. How is the *bouquet* in the story different from the *bouquet* described in the dictionary definition?

It is not made of flowers, it is made of gold, bread, and salt.

UNIT 5 Storytelling • **Lesson 5** *The Keeping Quilt*

▶ **Words with Foreign Origins**

Practice

Find the word *handkerchief* on page 160 of "The Keeping Quilt" and think about how context clues, related words, the base word, and a dictionary can help you discover its meaning.

4. Read the sentence that contains the word *handkerchief.*

5. What are some context clues within the surrounding sentences that can help you understand the meaning of a *handkerchief*?

possible clue words: linen, hankie, tied into

6. Circle the base word *kerchief* in the word *handkerchief.*
hand(kerchief)

7. What is the dictionary definition for the word *kerchief*?

cloth worn over the head or around the neck

8. What is a possible meaning of a *handkerchief*?

possible definition: a type of cloth you hold

in your hand

9. The word *chief* comes from a French word, meaning "head." What is the definition for the word *handkerchief* in the dictionary?

a piece of cloth used to wipe the face or head

VOCABULARY

The /kw/ and /skw/ Sounds

Word List

1. quit
2. quack
3. quick
4. quiet
5. quite
6. squid
7. squint
8. squirt
9. square
10. squeak
11. question
12. squeeze
13. squirrel
14. quality

Selection Words

15. quilt

Pattern Study

The **/kw/** sound is spelled **qu** as in *quick*. The **/skw/** sound is spelled **squ** as in *squirt*. In English, *q* is always followed by *u*.

▶ Sort the spelling words under the correct heading.

order of answers may vary

Words with the /kw/ Sound	Words with the /skw/ Sound
1. quit	9. squid
2. quack	10. squint
3. quick	11. squirt
4. quiet	12. square
5. quite	13. squeak
6. question	14. squeeze
7. quality	15. squirrel
8. quilt	

UNIT 5 Storytelling • **Lesson 5** *The Keeping Quilt*

▶ **The /kw/ and /skw/ Sounds**

Strategies

Visualization Strategy Circle the correctly spelled words. Write the correct spellings on the lines provided.

16. quac   (quack)   **quack**

17. (quiet)   queit   **quiet**

18. squeek   (squeak)   **squeak**

19. squirel   (squirrel) **squirrel**

20. (question) questun   **question**

Rhyming Strategy Write the spelling word that rhymes with each word below.

21. share **square**   24. speak **squeak**

22. guilt **quilt**   25. shirt **squirt**

23. sneeze **squeeze**

Meaning Strategy Write the spelling word next to its meaning clue.

26. stop trying   **quit**

27. fast; rapid   **quick**

28. a shape with four equal sides   **square**

29. small animal with bushy tail   **squirrel**

SPELLING

UNIT 5 Storytelling • **Lesson 6** *Johnny Appleseed*

▶ Prefixes

Remember, a prefix is a part added to the beginning of a base word that changes the meaning of the word.

Prefix (Meaning)	+ Base Word	= New Word	New Meaning
un- ("not or opposite of")	+ *tie*	= *untie*	"opposite of tying"
re- ("again")	+ *write*	= *rewrite*	"write again"

 **Notice how the word *untamed*, on page 174 of "Johnny Appleseed," contains the prefix *un-*.**

1. Circle the base word *tame* in the word *untamed* below:

   un(tame)d

2. What does the word *tame* mean? Look in a dictionary if you are unsure.

   not wild; domesticated; trained; under control

3. Since you know that the prefix *un-* means "not" or "opposite of," what does the word *untamed* mean?

   possible answer: not tamed; wild; untrained

4. What context clues from the story also help you learn the meaning of *untamed?*

   wilderness; survival; land; wolf

▶ **Prefixes**

VOCABULARY

Practice

Remember, prefixes are added to the beginnings of words and change the meanings of words. Write words with prefixes that match the meaning clues below. Look on page 58 if you need help with the meanings of the prefixes.

Find the word *recollections* on page 174 of "Johnny Appleseed."

5. Circle the base word *collect* in the word *recollections* below:
re(collect)ions

6. What does the word *collect* mean? Look in a dictionary if you are unsure.

to gather together

7. Since you know that the prefix *re-* means "again," what does the word *recollection* mean?

possible answer: to gather together again

8. What is the definition for *recollections* in the dictionary?

things recalled in the mind; memories

9. What context clues from the story also help you learn the meaning of *recollections?*

folks remembered him; retold stories

UNIT 5 Storytelling • **Lesson 6** *Johnny Appleseed*

The /s/ and /j/ Sounds

Word List

1. since
2. sauce
3. safe
4. sink
5. nice
6. gym
7. germ
8. magic
9. age
10. gentle

Selection Words

11. hinge
12. cellar
13. second
14. cider
15. largest

order of
answers
may vary

Pattern Study

The /s/ sound is often spelled with an *s* as in *safe*. The /s/ sound can also be spelled *c* when it is followed by the letters *i, e,* or *y,* as in *city*.

The /j/ sound can be spelled *g* before the letters *i, e,* or *y,* as in *germ*.

▶ Sort the spelling words under the correct heading.

/s/ spelled *s*

1. since
2. sauce
3. safe
4. sink
5. second

/s/ spelled *c*

6. since
7. sauce
8. nice
9. cellar
10. cider

/j/ spelled *ge*

11. gentle
12. age
13. germ
14. hinge

/j/ spelled *gi* or *gy*

15. magic
16. gym

UNIT 5 Storytelling • **Lesson 6** *Johnny Appleseed*

▶ **The /s/ and /j/ Sounds**

SPELLING

Strategies

Rhyming Strategy Write the spelling words that rhyme with the given words.

17. prince   **since**   20. term   **germ**

18. wink   **sink**   21. page   **age**

19. rider   **cider**

Meaning Strategy Write the spelling word next to its meaning clue.

22. protected, out of danger   **safe**

23. comes after first   **second**

24. opposite of smallest   **largest**

25. kind; sweet   **nice**

26. something poured on food   **sauce**

Visualization Strategy Look at each word below. If the word is spelled correctly, write the word *correct* on the line. If the word is misspelled, write the correct spelling on the line.

27. hinge   **correct**   30. gentle   **correct**

28. celler   **cellar**   31. lardgest   **largest**

29. aig   **age**

Unit 5 Review

Remember, you can learn a lot more about a word by linking it to types or categories. Remember, a **category** is a group of things that all have some of the same features.

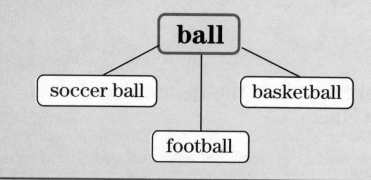

ball

soccer ball   basketball

football

Try It!   **Find the word *terrapins* on page 183 of "Aunt Flossie's Hats."**

1. What else is sold in the store besides *terrapins*? crabs

2. Find the definition of a *terrapin* in the dictionary. Fill in the blank in the word map to show the meaning of *terrapins*.

definition: **a turtle that lives near fresh water in North America**

turtles

fresh water turtles

terrapins

UNIT 5 Storytelling • **Lesson 7** *Aunt Flossie's Hats*

▶**Unit 5 Review**

VOCABULARY

Practice

Remember, homographs are words that are spelled alike but have different pronunciations and different meanings.

Find the word *minute* on page 181 of "Aunt Flossie's Hats." The words *minute* and *minute* are homographs.

3. Spell the two words: _____minute_____ _____minute_____

Do they have the same spelling? _____yes_____

4. What is the meaning of the word *minute* in the context of the sentence below?
"Aunt Flossie almost always thinks a *minute* before she starts a hat story."

minute: _____60 seconds, some time_____

5. Circle how the word *minute* is pronounced in the sentence above.
(min'it)   mī noot'

6. What is the meaning of the word *minute* in the context of the sentence below?
Detectives look for *minute* clues like dust and fingerprints.

minute: _____tiny; small; careful_____

7. Circle how the word *minute* is pronounced in the sentence above.
min'it   (mī noot')

UNIT 5 Storytelling • **Lesson 7** *Aunt Flossie's Hats*

Unit 5 Review

Word List

1. police
2. wrote
3. plunge
4. huge
5. quake
6. seven
7. shelf
8. city
9. stripe
10. spray

Selection Words

11. racing
12. wrestle
13. buttons
14. story
15. engines

Pattern Study

The spelling words review the spelling patterns learned throughout Unit 5.

> Consonant Blends
> /n/ spelled *kn_* and /r/ spelled *wr_*
> Words with *lf*, *mb*, and *tch*
> The /ə/ Sound
> The /kw/ and /skw/ Sounds
> The /s/ and /j/ Sounds

▶ Sort the spelling words under the correct heading.
order of answers may vary

Words with /r/ spelled *wr_*

1. **wrote**   2. **wrestle**

Words with the /j/ sound spelled *g* or *ge*

3. **engines**   4. **plunge**   5. **huge**

Words with /s/ spelled *ce* or *ci*

6. **police**   7. **city**   8. **racing**

Word with the /kw/ sound

9. **quake**

Words with *spr*, *st*, or *str*

10. **spray**   11. **stripe**   12. **story**

UNIT 5 Storytelling • **Lesson 7** *Aunt Flossie's Hats*

▶ **Unit 5 Review**

SPELLING

Strategies

Visualization Strategy Circle and then write the spelling word that is spelled correctly.

13. wroet   (wrote)   **wrote**

14. (huge)   hudge   **huge**

15. rasing   (racing)   **racing**

16. buttuns   (buttons)   **buttons**

17. (engines)   enjenes   **engines**

Rhyming Strategy Write the spelling word that rhymes with each word below.

18. eleven   **seven**   20. pity   **city**

19. rake   **quake**   21. note   **wrote**

Consonant-Substitution Strategy Substitute the given consonants for the underlined consonants in each word. Write the new word on the line.

22. stri<u>p</u>e (k)   **strike**   25. <u>sh</u>elf (s)   **self**

23. <u>sp</u>ray (t)   **stray**   26. <u>qu</u>ake (l)   **lake**

24. <u>r</u>acing (p)   **pacing**

UNIT 6 Country Life • **Lesson I** *The Country Mouse and the City Mouse*

Antonyms

Remember, **antonyms** are words that have opposite meanings. The story "The Country Mouse and the City Mouse" has many words that are antonyms because the two mice have very different lives.

The words *rich* and *poor* from the story are antonyms because they have opposite meanings.

> *rich* "having a lot of money"
> *poor* "having very little money"

 **Answer the questions below.**

1. Notice *city* in the title "The Country Mouse and the City Mouse." What type of mouse is the opposite of a *city mouse?*

   a country mouse

2. What word in the title is an antonym of *city?*

   country

3. Think of how *city* and *country* can have opposite meanings. List some things that could be found in the *city* that would not be found in the *country*.

   traffic, skyscrapers, parking lots, subways

Antonyms • Spelling and Vocabulary Skills

▶ Antonyms

Practice

Read the sentence below from "The Country Mouse and the City Mouse" that has the word *luxury* in it.

A simple life in peace and safety is preferable to a life of luxury tortured by fear.

4. What does the sentence say about a "life of luxury"?

possible answer: a life of luxury is

one that involves fear

5. What does it say about a "simple life"?

possible answer: a simple life is

peaceful and safe

6. Look up the words *luxury* and *simple* in a dictionary. Write the definitions below:

luxury: gives comfort, excess

simple (as the opposite of luxury): plain, without anything added

7. Are the words *luxury* and *simple* synonyms or antonyms? How do you know?

they are antonyms because they

have opposite meanings

VOCABULARY

Irregular Plurals

Word List

1. deer
2. geese
3. fish
4. wolves
5. leaves
6. loaves
7. scarves
8. selves
9. shelves
10. calves
11. sheep
12. shrimp
13. wives

Selection Words

14. mice
15. lives

Order of answers may vary

Pattern Study

Words that end in *f* or *fe* change the *f* to *v* and add *-es* or *-s* to form plurals.

wol*f*, wol*ves*   li*fe*, li*ves*

Some words, such as *deer*, have the same singular and plural forms.

Some words, such as *goose* and *geese*, change spellings in the plural form.

▶ Sort the spelling words under the correct heading. Change the *f* to *v* and add *-es*.

1. leaves   5. selves
2. scarves   6. shelves
3. wolves   7. calves
4. loaves

Change the *fe* to *v* and add *-es*.

8. wives   9. lives

Words with spelling changes

10. geese   11. mice

UNIT 6 Country Life • **Lesson I** *The Country Mouse and the City Mouse*

► **Irregular Plurals**

Strategies

Visualization Strategy Circle the correct spelling for each word. Write the correct spelling on the line.

12. (wolves)   wolfes   **wolves** _____

13. lifes   (lives)   **lives** _____

14. sheeps   (sheep)   **sheep** _____

15. selfs   (selves)   **selves** _____

16. (mice)   mices   **mice** _____

Meaning Strategy Write the spelling word that correctly completes each phrase.

17. one deer   many **deer** _____

18. a scarf   two **scarves** _____

19. one shrimp   a dozen **shrimp** _____

20. a leaf   a tree full of **leaves** _____

21. one goose   many **geese** _____

22. a small calf   a group of **calves** _____

23. a wife   many **wives** _____

24. one wolf   a pack of **wolves** _____

25. a shelf   a closet full of **shelves** _____

SPELLING

UNIT 6   Country Life • **Lesson 2** *Heartland*

Synonyms

Remember, **synonyms** are words with the same or nearly the same meanings, such as *laugh* and *giggle*.

If you know a synonym for a word, you can begin to understand the meaning of the word by replacing the synonym for the word in the sentence.

Example: People <u>smile</u> when they are happy.
People <u>grin</u> when they are happy.

 **Try It!**   **Find the word *toil* on page 207 of "Heartland."**

1. Read the line with the word *toil*. What do farmers do "throughout the season"?

   they toil

2. Read the next two lines. What do the farmers do "hard and long"?

   work

3. What could be a synonym for *toil?*

   work

4. Look in a dictionary to find one more synonym for the verb *toil*.

   possible synonyms: labor, strive

▶ **Synonyms**

Practice

Find the word *earth* **on page 210 of "Heartland."**
Read the sentence in which the word is found.

5. Write some words from the sentence that could be
   context clues to help you learn the meaning of the
   word.

   possible answers: rich, dark, fields, yields

6. Since the word *earth* is not capitalized, we can tell
   the author does not mean the planet Earth. What
   do you think *earth* means in the sentence?

   the ground, the dirt, the soil

7. Find two synonyms for the word *earth* in a
   thesaurus or a dictionary to see if your definition is
   correct.

   possible answers: soil, land, dirt, ground

8. Substitute your synonyms for the word *earth* in the
   sentences below. **Answers may vary.**

   The gardener planted flowers in the rich <u>earth</u>.

   The gardener planted flowers in the rich _____
   ground, soil, dirt, land

   The gardener planted flowers in the rich **soil** _____

   _____ .

VOCABULARY

UNIT 6 Country Life • **Lesson 2** *Heartland*

Double Consonants + y

Word List

1. dizzy
2. hilly
3. messy
4. foggy
5. soggy
6. sunny
7. bunny
8. funny
9. guppy
10. puppy
11. smelly
12. sloppy
13. silly

Selection Words

14. chilly
15. grassy

Pattern Study

Most double consonants are found in the middle or at the end of a word. In this lesson, look for double consonants in words that have a short vowel sound and end in *y*, as in *messy*, *funny*, and *silly*.

▶ Sort the spelling words with double consonants + *y* under the correct heading. **Order of answers may vary.**

Words with double *n* + *y*

1. __sunny__   2. __bunny__   3. __funny__

Words with double *p* + *y*

4. __guppy__   5. __puppy__   6. __sloppy__

Words with double *g* + *y*

7. __foggy__   8. __soggy__

Words with double *l* + *y*

9. __hilly__   10. __smelly__

11. __chilly__   12. __silly__

Words with double *s* + *y*

13. __messy__   14. __grassy__

Name _____ Date _____

SPELLING

▶ **Double Consonants + y**

Strategies

Rhyming Strategy Write the spelling word or words that rhyme with each word below.

Order of answers may vary.

15. runny   sunny   funny   bunny

16. frizzy   dizzy

17. frilly   chilly   hilly

Meaning Strategy Write the spelling word that correctly completes each sentence.

18. A __sunny__ day is perfect for a picnic.

19. Clowns can make __silly or funny__ faces that make us laugh.

20. Roller coasters make some people feel __dizzy__.

21. You wear a coat when it is __chilly__ outside.

Visualization Strategy Circle and then write the spelling word that is spelled correctly.

22. smely   (smelly)   smelly

23. (foggy)   fogy   foggy

24. chily   (chilly)   chilly

25. (soggy)   sogy   soggy

UNIT 6 Country Life • **Lesson 3** *Leah's Pony*

Homophones

Remember, **homophones** are words that sound alike but have different spellings and different meanings.

Example: *hear* and *here* are homophones

The words sound alike: *hear here*
The words have different spellings: *hear here*
The words have different meanings:

> *hear* (to receive sound through the ears)
> *here* (at, in, or to this place)

To spell homophones correctly, you must know the context in which the word is being used.

> Can you *hear* what I am saying?
> Please come *here* and see the painting.

 **Read the sentence with *sell* from page 221 of "Leah's Pony."**

1. What is the meaning of *sell* in the sentence?

possible answer: offer something to be bought

2. The words *sell* and *cell* are homophones. How do you know?

Do they sound alike? **yes** _____

Write the two different spellings: **sell** _____ **cell** _____

Write the two different definitions:

sell: **to give something in return for money**

cell: **possible answer: a small room or space**

UNIT 6 Country Life • **Lesson 3** *Leah's Pony*

▶ **Homophones**

Practice

The word *cheap* on page 227 of "Leah's Pony" sounds like the word *cheep*. Are these two words homophones? How do you know?

3. Spell the two words: __cheep__   __cheap__

4. What is the meaning of *cheap* in the sentence?
__not expensive; costing little money__

5. What does the word *cheep* mean?
__a high-pitched sound made by chicks__

Complete the sentences below with the homophone pairs. Make sure to write the correct word in the blank that makes sense in the context of the sentence.

zHomophones

6. The dog didn't __hear__ his owner

shout, "Come __here__!"

here, hear

7. She wants __to__ eat

__two__ chocolate cookies.

two, to

8. They looked across the __sea__

to __see__ the boats pass.

see, sea

9. You can go __by__ the grocery store

to __buy__ some food.

by, buy

road, rode

VOCABULARY

Words with -er and -est

Word List

1. dizzier
2. happier
3. heavier
4. hungrier
5. prettier
6. drowsier
7. greater
8. greatest
9. dizziest
10. drowsiest
11. happiest
12. heaviest
13. hungriest

Selection Words

14. finest
15. taller

Order of answers may vary.

Pattern Study

The endings **-er** and **-est** are added to words to show comparisons, such as *greater* and *greatest*. The **-er** ending usually means "more," and the **-est** ending usually means "most." Drop the silent *e* before adding these endings to words such as *fin<u>er</u>* and *fin<u>est</u>*. If a word ends in *y*, change the *y* to *i* before adding **-er** or **-est**.

happy	happi<u>er</u>	happi<u>est</u>

▶ Sort the spelling words under the correct heading.

Words with -est

1. dizziest
2. greatest
3. drowsiest
4. happiest
5. heaviest
6. hungriest
7. finest

Words with -er

8. dizzier
9. happier
10. heavier
11. hungrier
12. prettier
13. greater
14. taller
15. drowsier

▶ **Words with -er and -est**

Strategies

 Visualization Strategy Circle the correct spelling for each word. Write the correct spelling on the line.

16. taler   (taller)   **taller** _____

17. drowsist   (drowsiest)   **drowsiest** _____

18. (dizzier)   dizzyer   **dizzier** _____

19. finist   (finest)   **finest** _____

20. (prettier)   pretier   **prettier** _____

 Meaning Strategy Write the spelling word that correctly matches the meaning clue.

21. more happy **happier** _____

22. the most heavy **heaviest** _____

23. the most fine **finest** _____

24. more pretty **prettier** _____

25. the most hungry **hungriest** _____

26. the most dizzy **dizziest** _____

27. the most happy **happiest** _____

28. the most great **greatest** _____

SPELLING

UNIT 6 Country Life • **Lesson 4** *Cows in the Parlor*

Categories

Remember, a **category** is a grouping of different types of things. The word map below can help you learn some types of balls.

```
      soccer ball              football


   tennis ball        balls          volleyball


              basketball
```

 **Try It!**   **Find bales on page 239 of "Cows in the Parlor."**

1. What is done to hay before it is made into bales?

it is cut and then dried

2. Find the definition of *bale* in a dictionary.

bale: **a large, tight bundle of things tied together**

3. The word map shows the steps for making bales of hay. Fill in the empty box.

grass ─ cut grass ─ dried grass ─ **hay** ─ bales of hay

UNIT 6 Country Life • **Lesson 4** *Cows in the Parlor*

▶ Categories

VOCABULARY

Practice

Find the word *silage* on page 240 of "Cows in the Parlor."

4. What is the word *silage* describing in the story?

A type of cattle feed made from <u>corn</u>

5. What has been done to the corn?

<u>the corn has been chopped and put in a silo</u>

6. What is silage used for in the story?

<u>to feed the farmer's cows</u>

7. Fill in the empty boxes in the word map.

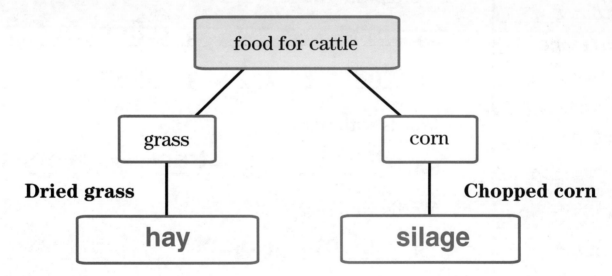

food for cattle

grass   corn

Dried grass   **Chopped corn**

hay   silage

UNIT 6 Country Life • **Lesson 4** *Cows in the Parlor*

Words with Latin Roots

Word List

1. collect
2. elect
3. select
4. report
5. sports
6. support
7. export
8. import
9. attract
10. subtract
11. fines
12. final
13. refine

Selection Words

14. tractor
15. finished

Order of answers may vary.

Pattern Study

Latin roots are word parts that have certain meanings.

The root **lect** means "gather," as in *collect*.
The root **port** means "carry," as in *report*.
The root **tract** means "pull or drag," as in the words *attract* and *tractor*.
The root **fin** means "end," as in *finish* and *final*.

▶ Sort the spelling words under the correct heading.
Words with **fin**

1. fines
2. final
3. refine
4. finished

Words with **tract**

5. attract
6. subtract
7. tractor

Words with **lect**

8. collect
9. elect
10. select

Words with **port**

11. report
12. sports
13. support
14. export
15. import

► **Words with Latin Roots**

SPELLING

Strategies

 Rhyming Strategy Write the spelling word or words that rhyme with each word below.

16. actor ___tractor___

17. lines ___fines___

18. forts ___sports___

 Visualization Strategy Circle and then write the spelling word that is spelled correctly.

19. colect (collect) ___collect___

20. ellect (elect) ___elect___

21. (support) suport ___support___

22. finel (final) ___final___

23. (subtract) subtrack ___subtract___

 Meaning Strategy Write the spelling word next to its meaning clue.

24. activities such as football and soccer ___sports___

25. to take away; not add ___subtract___

26. to choose ___select___

UNIT 6 Country Life • **Lesson 5** *Just Plain Fancy*

Base Word Families

A **base word** is a word that can have prefixes, suffixes, and endings added to it. **Base word families** are all the related words you can make with that base word. If you know the meaning of the base word, you can begin to better understand the meanings of all its related words.

Base Word	Related Words
friend	*friendly, befriend, unfriendly*

 **Try It!** **Notice the vocabulary word *unharnessed* on page 251 of "Just Plain Fancy."**

1. Circle the word *harness* hidden in the word *unharnessed* below:

un(harness)ed

2. What does it mean to harness a horse? Find the definition in a dictionary if you do not know.

harness: **to put straps and bands, or a harness, on a horse so it can do work**

3. What does it mean if someone unharnessed a horse, like the father in the story did? (Remember, ***un-*** is a prefix meaning "the opposite of.")

possible answer: the straps and bands, or harness, were taken off the horse

UNIT 6 Country Life • **Lesson 5** *Just Plain Fancy*

▶ **Base Word Families**

VOCABULARY

Practice

Remember, words in the same base word family have meanings related to one base word. In the groups of words below, circle the two words that are in the same base word family. Write the base word of each group on the line.

Base Word

4. (wooden) (woodwork) woolen   **wood**

5. nearly (nervous) (nerves)   **nerve**

6. (happily) hallway (happiness)   **happy**

7. (colorful) (colorless) close   **color**

8. (corrected) corner (incorrect)   **correct**

9. (harmful) (unharmed) hearty   **harm**

10. (spelling) sorrow (misspelled)   **spell**

UNIT 6 Country Life • **Lesson 5** *Just Plain Fancy*

Words with Greek Roots

Word List

1. critic
2. critical
3. criticize
4. phone
5. earphone
6. headphone
7. telephone
8. cent
9. center
10. central
11. century
12. cycle
13. bicycle
14. tricycle
15. unicycle

Order of answers may vary.

Pattern Study

Greek roots are word parts that have certain meanings.

The root **crit** means "judge," as in *critic*.
The root **phone** means "sound," as in *earphone*.
The root **cent** means "center," as in *center*.
The root **cycl** means "circle," as in *bicycle*.

▶ Sort the spelling roots under the correct heading.

Words with **cent**

1. cent   3. central
2. center   4. century

Words with **crit**

5. critic   6. criticize   7. critical

Words with **phon**

8. phone   10. headphone
9. earphone   11. telephone

Words with **cycl**

12. cycle   14. tricycle
13. bicycle   15. unicycle

UNIT 6 Country Life • **Lesson 5** *Just Plain Fancy*

▶ Words with Greek Roots

Strategies

Visualization Strategy Circle the correct spelling for each word. Write the correct spelling on the line.

16. (critical) criticle   critical

17. earfone (earphone)   earphone

18. bicicle (bicycle)   bicycle

19. (central) centrel   central

20. critisize (criticize)   criticize

Meaning Strategy Write the Greek root next to its meaning clue.

21. center   cent

22. circle   cycl

23. sound   phon

24. judge   crit

Meaning Strategy Write the spelling word next to its meaning clue.

25. the middle   center

26. one hundred years century

27. has three wheels   tricycle

SPELLING

Word Concept

Remember, the **concept** of a word is the general idea of the word. You can discover the concept of a word by thinking of related words or finding context clues.

Example: rotation (p. 263)

Related Words: rotate

Context Clues: ". . . corn one year and barley the next."

Concept: *rotation* has to do with how something changes or its pattern

 **Try It!** **Read the sentence containing the word *mortgage* from page 272 of "What Ever Happened to the Baxter Place?"**

1. List two or more words related to *mortgage.*

possible answers: owed, house, borrowed

2. According to the story, what had a mortgage on it?

the house

3. Who did the Baxters owe for the mortgage? **the bank**

4. What could be the concept of the word *mortgage?*

something like a loan for a house owed to a bank

5. Find the meaning of *mortgage* in the dictionary.

money owed on property or a loan on property

▶ **Word Concept**

VOCABULARY

Practice

Find the word *partial* on page 274 of "What Ever Happened to the Baxter Place?" Read the sentence in which the word is found. Discovering the concept of the word can help you learn what the word means in the sentence.

6. Find the base word in *partial*.

part

7. What does it mean to get part of something?

not to get all of it

8. Find the word *partial* in a dictionary and write the definition below:

possible definition: not complete; not total

9. Find the word *scholarship* in a dictionary and write the definition below:

possible definition: money given to pay for studies

10. Thinking about the base word and the two definitions, describe the concept of a "partial scholarship," as used in the story.

answers will vary: some money paid for studies, but not all

Words with Foreign Origins

Word List

1. hamster
2. hamburger
3. yodel
4. pretzel
5. trio
6. alto
7. tempo
8. plaza
9. armadillo
10. cafe
11. collage
12. bouquet

Selection Words

13. mortgage
14. alfalfa
15. boutique

Answers may vary.

Pattern Study

Many German words have the /er/ sound or end with the /əl/ sound spelled *-el*.

> hamburg<u>er</u>   yod<u>el</u>

Many French words end in *-e, -et, -age,* or *-que*. The *-e* and *-et* spellings make the /ā/ sound.

> caf<u>e</u>   coll<u>age</u>   bouti<u>que</u>

Many Spanish and Italian words end in vowels.

> temp<u>o</u>   plaz<u>a</u>   armadill<u>o</u>

▶ Sort the spelling words under the correct heading.

Two German words with /er/

1. **hamster** _____   2. **hamburger** _____

Two Spanish or Italian words ending with **o**

3. **trio** _____   4. **alto** _____

Two French words ending with **-age**

5. **collage** _____   6. **mortgage** _____

UNIT 6 Country Life • **Lesson 6** *What Ever Happened to the Baxter Place?*

► Words with Foreign Origins

Strategies

Visualization Strategy Circle and then write the spelling word that is spelled correctly.

7. (hamster) hamstar **hamster** _____

8. altoe (alto) **alto** _____

9. (plaza) plasa **plaza** _____

10. mortage (mortgage) **mortgage** _____

11. collague (collage) **collage** _____

Meaning Strategy Write the correct spelling word next to its meaning clue.

12. the musical beat or rhythm **tempo** _____

13. a grouping of flowers **bouquet** _____

14. green sprouts **alfalfa** _____

15. ground beef **hamburger** _____

16. twisted, baked bread **pretzel** _____

SPELLING

Unit 6 Review

Remember, **synonyms** are words with the same or nearly the same meanings, such as *mad* and *irate*. A dictionary or a thesaurus can help you find synonyms for many words.

Example: The girl was <u>mad</u> when someone stole her lunch.

The girl was <u>irate</u> when someone stole her lunch.

 **Try It!** Find the word *grit* on page 292 of "If you're not from the prairie . . . ."

1. Read the line with the word *grit*. What does the story say about grit? <u>it fills the eyes</u>

2. The word *grit* means small bits of sand. What could be a synonym for *grit*? <u>sand, dirt, soil</u>

3. Write a synonym for *grit* in the phrase from the story below:

"My eyes filled with <u>sand, dirt, soil</u> . . ."

UNIT 6 Country Life • **Lesson 7** *If you're not from the prairie . . .*

▶**Unit 6 Review**

Practice

The word *through* on page 287 of "If you're not from the prairie . . ." sounds like the word *threw*.

4. Spell the two words: <u>through</u> <u>threw</u>

5. What is the meaning of the word *through* in the context of the sentence in the story? Check in a dictionary if you are unsure.

<u>from beginning to end, from one side to the other</u>

6. What does the word *threw* mean?

<u>to have thrown something; tossed</u>

7. Are these two words homophones? How do you know?

<u>they sound the same, but have different spellings and meanings</u>

Complete the sentences below with *through* or *threw*. Make sure to write the correct word in the blank that makes sense in the context of the sentence.

8. The pitcher <u>threw</u> a curveball to the batter.

9. The ball shot <u>through</u> the catcher's glove and into the dugout.

10. The teammates <u>threw</u> up their hats at the amazing pitch.

VOCABULARY

UNIT 6 Country Life • **Lesson 7** *If you're not from the prairie . . .*

Unit 6 Review

Word List

1. knives
2. trout
3. airport
4. flurry
5. dirtiest
6. prettiest
7. sillier
8. ballet
9. earphones
10. cycling
11. cleaner

Selection Words

12. children
13. messages
14. brighter
15. brightest

Order of answers may vary.

Pattern Study

The spelling words in this lesson review irregular plurals, double consonants + *y*, adding **-er** or **-est**, Latin roots, Greek roots, and spelling patterns from other languages.

▶ Find the spelling word with a double consonant + *y*.

1. **flurry** _____

▶ Find the spelling word in which *f* changed to *v* and -*s* was added.

2. **knives** _____

▶ Find the spelling words with **-er** or **-est**.

3. **dirtiest** _____
4. **prettiest** _____
5. **sillier** _____
6. **cleaner** _____
7. **brighter** _____
8. **brightest** _____

▶ Find the spelling word with the same singular and plural form.

9. **trout** _____

Strategies

 Rhyming Strategy Write the spelling word or words that rhyme with each word below.

10. wives **knives**

11. fighter **brighter**

12. hurry **flurry**

 Meaning Strategy Write the spelling word that correctly completes each sentence.

13. In _____**ballet**_____, the dancer is very graceful.

14. Some people choose _____**cycling**_____ as a form of exercise.

15. Airplanes take off from an _____**airport**_____ .

16. Most _____**children**_____ take their favorite toy when going on a long trip.

 Visualization Strategy Circle and then write the spelling word that is spelled correctly.

17. (airport)   airpert   **airport**

18. dirtyest   (dirtiest)   **dirtiest**

19. mesages   (messages)   **messages**

Vocabulary Rules

Synonyms are words that are similar in meaning.

The solution to the puzzle is **easy.**
The solution to the puzzle is **simple.**

Antonyms are words that are opposite in meaning.

An elephant is a **large** animal.
A mouse is a **small** animal.

Homophones are words that are pronounced alike but are spelled differently and have different meanings.

The wind **blew** white clouds across the **blue** sky.
They're happy that **their** team won over **there.**
You're sure **your** team won?
It's a shame that the tree lost **its** leaves so soon.

Context Clues

When you come to a new word in your reading, you can sometimes figure out the meaning of the word from its context, the words and sentences around it. Writers give context clues in five main ways.

▶ **Definition** The meaning of the word is stated.

Mother ordered a *cushion*, which is a **soft pillow.**

▶ **Example** The meaning of the unfamiliar word is explained through examples.

Her *interjections*—**Ouch! Wow!**—are so dramatic.

▶ **Comparison** The unfamiliar word is similar to a familiar word or phrase.

Why would I *retract* my statement? I will not **withdraw** it.

▶ **Contrast** The unfamiliar word is opposite a familiar word or phrase.

She is really a *novice*, although she appears **experienced.**

▶ **Cause and Effect** The unfamiliar word is explained as part of a cause-and-effect relationship.

He really enjoyed the *hors d'oeuvres* tonight because he always has a **snack** before dinner.

VOCABULARY

Prefixes and Suffixes

- **Prefixes** are word parts added to the beginning of a root that change its meaning.

    A **co**worker is a person with whom one works.
    To **co**write is to write together.

- **Suffixes** are word parts added to the end of a root to change its meaning.

    Fear**ful** means "full of fear."
    A spoon**ful** is the amount that fills a spoon.

Word Roots

A word root is the main part of a word. Sometimes a prefix or suffix is added to it. These additions often change a word's meaning or its part of speech.

    Audio means "hear."

    An **audiotape** is a tape you **listen** to.
    An **audience** is a group that **hears** a performance.
    Audiovisual materials help us see and **hear** what we are learning.

Multiple-Meaning Words

Multiple-meaning words are words that have the same spelling and pronunciation but have more than one meaning and may be different parts of speech in different situations.

> **Gorge**
> **Noun:** a deep, narrow valley with steep sides
> **Verb:** to eat greedily

Analogies

An analogy compares two pairs of words. The relationship between the two words in the first pair is the same as the relationship between the words in the second pair.

- One kind of analogy shows the relationship between **synonyms**, or words close in meaning.

   > **Happy** is to **glad** as **sad** is to **downcast.**
   > (**Happy** and **glad** are synonyms, and **sad** and **downcast** are synonyms.)

- Another kind of analogy shows the relationship between **antonyms,** or words that are opposite in meaning.

   > **Hard** is to **soft** as **friends** are to **enemies.**
   > (**Hard** and **soft** are antonyms as are **friends** and **enemies.**)

- A third kind of analogy involves one term describing something about the other term.

   > **Dog** is to **bark** as **cat** is to **meow.**
   > (This analogy is describing sounds: A **dog barks** while a **cat meows.**)

Spelling Strategies

There are many different ways to learn how to spell. A spelling strategy is a plan that can make learning to spell easier. Take some time to learn how these strategies can help you spell better.

Sound Pattern Strategies

Pronunciation Strategy
Learn to listen to the sounds in a word. Then spell each sound. *(sit)*

Consonant-Substitution Strategy
Try switching consonant letters without changing the vowel. *(bat, hat, rat, flat, splat)*

Vowel-Substitution Strategy
Try switching the vowel letters without changing the rest of the word. *(hit, hat, hut, hot)* / *(mane, mine)*

Rhyming Strategy
Think of a word that rhymes with the spelling word and has the same spelling pattern. *(cub, tub, rub)*

Structural Pattern Strategies

Conventions Strategy
Think about the rules and exceptions you have learned for adding endings to words. *(crying, cried)*

Visualization Strategy
Think about how the word looks. Most words look wrong when they do not have the right spelling. *(can,* not *cen)*

Proofreading Strategy
Check your writing carefully for spelling mistakes.

Meaning Pattern Strategies

Family Strategy
Think of how words from the same family are spelled. *(art, artist)*

Meaning Strategy
Think about the meaning of the word to make sure you're using the right word. *(see, sea)*

Compound Word Strategy
Break the compound into its two words to spell each word. *(homework, home work)*

Foreign Language Strategy
Think of foreign word spellings that are different from English spelling patterns. *(ballet)*

Dictionary Strategy
Find the word in a dictionary to make sure your spelling is correct.

Spelling Rules

General Spelling Rules for Most Words

- All words have at least one vowel.

- Most words have at least one consonant.

- Every syllable has a vowel or the letter *y*.

- Many words are spelled exactly as they sound.

- Some words are exceptions to spelling rules and must be memorized.

Consonant Spellings

Most consonants sound like their letter names.

- /b/ is spelled *b* as in *bad*
- /d/ is spelled *d* as in *dash*
- /f/ is spelled *f* as in *fast*
- /j/ is spelled *j* as in *jog*
- /k/ is spelled *k* as in *kiss*
- /l/ is spelled *l* as in *lot*
- /m/ is spelled *m* as in *map*
- /n/ is spelled *n* as in *nest*
- /p/ is spelled *p* as in *pin*
- /r/ is spelled *r* as in *rug*
- /s/ is spelled *s* as in *sand*
- /t/ is spelled *t* as in *tip*
- /v/ is spelled *v* as in *vat*
- /z/ is spelled *z* as in *zip*

Consonant Spellings

Some consonants do not sound like their letter names.

- /h/ does not sound like the letter *h*. *(hill)*
- /w/ does not sound like the letter *w*. *(wish)*
- /y/ does not sound like the letter *y*. *(yell)*

- There are hard and soft sounds for the letter *c*.
    hard *c:* /k/ is spelled *c* as in *can*
    soft *c:* /s/ is spelled *c* as in *cell*

- There are hard and soft sounds for the letter *g*.
    hard *g:* /g/ is spelled *g* as in *gum*
    soft *g:* /j/ is spelled *g* as in *gym*

- The /ks/ as in *ax* or the /gz/ as in *exact* are both spelled with the letter *x*.

Consonant Blends

Consonant blends are two- or three-letter combinations in which each letter can be heard.

- Three main groupings are the *s*-blends, *r*-blends, and *l*-blends.

- Two-letter *s*-blend /sl/ is spelled *sl* as in <u>*sl*ip</u>
  /sp/ is spelled *sp* as in <u>*sp*eak</u>
  /sk/ is spelled *sk* as in <u>*sk*y</u>
  /sk/ is spelled *sc* as in <u>*sc*are</u>
  /sm/ is spelled *sm* as in <u>*sm*ell</u>
  /sn/ is spelled *sn* as in <u>*sn*ow</u>
  /st/ is spelled *st* as in <u>*st*ack</u>
  /sw/ is spelled *sw* as in <u>*sw*im</u>

- The blends *sc* and *sk* both spell the /sk/ sound. *(scan, skip)*

- When you hear the /sk/ sound at the end of a word, spell it *sk*, not *sc*. *(risk, not risc)*

- Only a few words have *sp* at the end, such as *wasp* and *lisp*.

Spelling Rules • Spelling and Vocabulary Skills

Consonant Blends

- Three-letter *s*-blend /skr/ is spelled <u>scr</u> as in *scream*
  /spl/ is spelled *spl* as in <u>spl</u>*it*
  /spr/ is spelled *spr* as in <u>spr</u>*ay*
  /str/ is spelled *str* as in *string*

- Blends found at the ends of words:
  /ft/ is spelled *ft* as in *gi<u>ft</u>*
  /lf/ is spelled *lf* as in *el<u>f</u>*
  /lp/ is spelled *lp* as in *hel<u>p</u>*
  /ld/ is spelled *ld* as in *bal<u>d</u>*
  /lk/ is spelled *lk* as in *mil<u>k</u>*
  /lt/ is spelled *lt* as in *wil<u>t</u>*

- The *l* is silent in *half* and *calf*.

- The final-consonant blends *mp*, *nd*, *ng*, *nk*, and *nt*
  are found at the end of one-syllable words. Most
  often, the vowel that comes before the blend has a
  short-vowel sound.

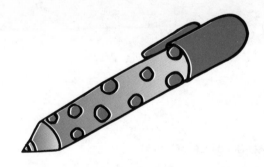

SHORT-VOWEL SOUND SPELLINGS

Short-vowel sound spellings are more predictable than long-vowel sound spellings.

- Short-vowel sounds most often are found in words beginning with a vowel, such as *up*, *at*, and *end*, or words with *vowel-consonant* endings, such as *cup*, *bat*, and *lend*.

- Some short-vowel sounds are spelled with two or more letters, such as *bread* and *laugh*.

- Short-vowels have many simple spelling patterns, such as *at*, *in*, *ot*, *et*, and *ug*.

The /a/ Sound
- /a/ is spelled *a*, as in *cat*.
- /a/ can also be spelled *au*, as in *laugh* or *ai* as in *plaid*.

The /e/ Sound
- /e/ is most often spelled *e*, as in *bed*.
- /e/ can be spelled *ea*, in the middle of a word, such as *bread* or *head*.

The /i/ Sound
- /i/ is most often spelled *i* as in *did*.
- When *y* is found in the middle of a word, it acts like a vowel. It usually makes the /i/ sound, as in *system*.
- /i/ is sometimes spelled *i_e*, as in the words *give* and *live*.

The /o/ Sound
- /o/ is usually spelled *o* as in *got*.
- /o/ can be spelled *o*, *oa*, *aw*, *au*, and *ou*, as in *dog*, *awful*, *broad*, *caught*, and *brought*.

Spelling Rules • Spelling and Vocabulary Skills

The /u/ Sound

- /u/ is usually spelled *u*, as in *fun*.
- /u/ can be spelled *o*, as in *son*, or *o_e*, as in *glove*, *love*, and *come*.

The /ow/ Sound

- /ow/ is spelled *ou*, as in *house*, or *ow* near the end of a word, as in *cow*.
- The *ou* spelling pattern occurs more often than the *ow* spelling.
- Sometimes the *ow* spelling can sound like the /ō/ sound.

The /oi/ Sound

- /oi/ is spelled *oy* or *oi*, as in *boy*, *oyster*, *boil*, and *oil*.
- The *oi* spelling is found at the beginning and in the middle of words.
- The *oy* spelling is mostly found at the end of a word and sometimes at the end of a syllable, as in *loyal*.

The /o͞o/ Sound

- /o͞o/ can be spelled *u* or *oo*, as in *pull* and *book*.
- In a few words, /o͞o/ can be spelled *ou*, as in *could*.

R-controlled Vowels

- Most *r*-controlled vowel sound spellings are found in words with just one syllable.
- The /ar/ sound can be spelled *ar* as in *car*. The /âr/ sound can be spelled *air* as in *chair*, *are* as in *care*, and *ear* as in *pear*.
- The /er/ sound can be spelled *er* as in *her*, *ir* as in *bird*, and *ur* as in *burn*.
- The /or/ sound can be spelled *or* as in *for*, *oar* as in *roar*, and *ore* as in *core*.

LONG-VOWEL SOUND SPELLINGS

Long vowels sound like the letter names.
When long-vowel sounds are spelled with two vowels, the first vowel is usually heard and the second vowel is silent.

Vowel-consonant-e

- Many long-vowel sounds have the common *vowel-consonant-e* spelling pattern in which the *e* is silent, as in the word *date*.

The /ā/ Sound

- /ā/ is spelled *a*, *a_e*, *ai*, and *ay*, as in *agent*, *base*, *raid*, and *today*. The *ay* spelling is found at the end of words, and the *ai* spelling is found in the middle of words.

The /ē/ Sound

- /ē/ is often spelled *e*, *e_e*, *ee*, *ea*, and *y* at the end of words such as *be*, *here*, *agree*, *easy*, and *happy*.
- /ē/ is spelled *ei* in a few words such as *receive*, but also *ie* as in *pierce*. Remember the rhyme: "Write *i* before *e*, except after *c*, or when it sounds like /ā/ as in *neighbor* and *weigh*."
- /ē/ is spelled *i_e* in some words, such as *machine*, *police*, *magazine*, and *trampoline*.

The /ī/ Sound

- /ī/ is spelled *i*, *i_e*, *igh*, and *y*, as in *icy*, *site*, *high*, *find*, and *dry*.

The /ō/ Sound

- /ō/ is spelled *o*, *o_e*, *oa*, and *ow*, as in *pony*, *bone*, *boat*, *revolt*, and *snow*.

The /ū/ Sound

- /ū/ is spelled *u*, *ue*, or *u_e*, as in *unit*, *argue*, and *cube*.

The /o͞o/ Sound

- /o͞o/ can be spelled *oo* in the middle of a word such as *tool*, *u* in the *u_e* pattern such as *tune*, or *ew* at the end of a word as in *new*.
- /o͞o/ can also be spelled *ough* in *through*.

STRUCTURAL SPELLING PATTERNS

Plurals
- Add -*s* to most nouns to make them plural.
  (*cat* + *s* = *cats*)
- Add -*es* to words that end in *ch*, *s*, *ss*, *x*, *z*, or *zz*.
- Noticing the syllables in the singular and plural forms of a word can help you know whether to add -*s* or -*es*. When -*es* is added, it usually adds another syllable.

Irregular Plurals
- For words that end in *f* or *fe*, change the *f* to a *v* and add -*es*.
- Some plurals are spelled the same as the singular form, like *deer*.
- The spelling changes in the plural form of some words, like *tooth* and *teeth*.
- For a word that ends in *consonant-o*, add -*es*. If a word ends in *vowel-o*, -*s* is usually added.

Adding Endings
- For most words, endings are simply added to the base words.
- If a word ends in *e* and the ending begins with a vowel, the *e* is dropped.
- When a word ends in *vowel-y*, just add the ending.